Foreword

By 2020, in large part due to the presence and efforts of Computing At School (CAS)[1] in England and Technocamps[2] in Wales, computing as an academic subject was required to be taught in schools. It was delivered in many (but not all) schools, and there was also extra-curricular activity, in the form of "code clubs", computing competitions and other events. In Scotland, computing continued to be part of the Secondary school curriculum offered in most schools in the 1990s and 2000s[3]. However, a rapid rise in the requirements for computing provision created issues with the supply and training of specialist educators and meant that there were relatively few qualified disciplinary computing teachers[4][5].

Universities have considerable interest and expertise in teaching computing, and there is quite a lot of engagement between schools and universities to support the learning of computing[6] in schools. In 2020, "quite a lot" was the best estimation that could be made. Outreach activities (where Universities reach outside of their core constituency of post-18 year old students) are long-established in some places. There are examples embedded into the undergraduate curriculum (as in "Student Ambassador" and "Computing in the Classroom" programmes), and some highly-structured offerings (such as Technocamps in Wales). But in the main, such activities tend to be local and largely invisible to each other.

The Council of Professors and Heads of Computing (CPHC) were interested in helping computing departments share these outreach practices and learn effective approaches from each other. To forward this, we created an "outreach network", commissioned a landscape survey to understand the nature and scope of activities, and at the same time organised a national workshop, with presentations of many forms of activity – almost exactly coincident with the arrival of COVID-19 and lockdown.

This report presents the results of the survey. The next steps for CPHC will be, as and when circumstances permit, to organise opportunities for sharing practice and collating case studies of effective and interesting approaches.

1 https://www.computingatschool.org.uk/
2 https://www.technocamps.com/en/
3 https://theferret.scot/computing-science-schools-scotland/
4 https://www.nfer.ac.uk/media/3784/retaining_science_mathematics_and_computing_teachers.pdf
5 https://royalsociety.org/-/media/policy/Publications/2019/21-08-19-policy-briefing-on-teachers-of-computing.pdf
6 We use "Computer Science" and "Computing" as a broad term: there is a wealth of 'computing' happening in other areas. These areas also have crossover with the digital media, ICT and iMedia courses that happen in school computing / IT / CS departments.

Opportunities

Opportunities

Our survey of 143 educators revealed both barriers and benefits for universities and schools in engaging with each other on computing education. We have synthesised a set of opportunities, grouped by stakeholders in the computing education landscape.

Universities with Computer Science departments could:

1. review how prior learning in computer science is taken into account when setting entry requirements and designing curricula and teaching materials: for example, requiring A level computing (see Section 4b);
2. promote the positive impact of outreach in schools to prospective and current students (See Section 1);
3. ensure that staff are properly recognised (in workload allocation models, or similar) for outreach work (See Section 1)

If they offer "outreach" activities they could:

1. provide appropriate administrative support to run outreach events (such as the Isaac Computing, LEGO League and the various Technocamps initiatives) (See Section 1).

If they include computing education modules with school placements they could:

1. provide appropriate administrative support (See Section 2);
2. review how all computer science students are taught to explain, support and teach others about programming. Learning how to teach others to program could increase student workplace readiness, boost teacher recruitment, and improve diversity and inclusion by influencing views of who has the ability to learn to program (see Section 2).

If they undertake computing education research they could:

1. engage in activities that include sharing research with teachers (See Section 3);
2. design and deliver professional development for Primary ITT lecturers with ITT specific resources (see Section 5);
3. investigate the quality of primary teachers' experience of computing in ITT and how this might be improved (see Section 5).

Universities that run Primary initial teacher training (ITT) programmes could:

1. investigate the quality of primary teachers' experience of computing in ITT and how this might be improved (see Section 5);
2. develop a community of practice amongst Primary ITT providers who have an interest in computing (see Section 5);
3. take part in Primary ITT computing research (see Section 5);
4. offer early-career enhancement courses on computing. This could match with recent DfE proposals for early-career enhancement[7] (see Section 5).

Universities that run Secondary initial teacher training (ITT) programmes could:

1. take part in Secondary ITT computing research (see Section 6);
2. offer early-career enhancement courses[8] on computing. This could match with recent DfE proposals for early-career enhancement[9] (see Section 6).
3. investigate how Secondary schools can be better matched with Secondary ITT universities and how mentors can be found to support trainees (see Section 6).

---

7 https://www.gov.uk/government/collections/early-career-framework-reforms
8 https://www.gov.uk/government/publications/teacher-recruitment-and-retention-strategy
9 https://www.gov.uk/government/collections/early-career-framework-reforms

Groups who develop computer educator professional development or computing classroom resources could:

1. promote the importance of computing education research by highlighting when material presented is research-led (see Section 4a and Section 4b);
2. create professional development offerings in computing education research (see Section 4a);
3. design and deliver professional development for Primary ITT lecturers with ITT specific resources (see Section 5).

Overseeing groups and others who support educators in computing education e.g. Council of Professors and Heads of Computing (CPHC)[10], BCS, the Chartered Institute for IT[11], Computing at School (CAS)[12], National Centre for Computing Education (NCCE)[13], STEM Learning[14], ACM UK SIGSCE (Special Interest Group in Computer Science Education)[15], Technocamps[16], Glow [17], could:

1. promote the positive impact of university schemes such as the Undergraduate Student Ambassador[18] program with schools, universities and students (See Section 2);
2. work with the Undergraduate Student Ambassador program to increase the profile of the scheme in computer science (See Section 2);
3. broker introductions between local schools and universities who want to run schemes (such as the Undergraduate Student Ambassadors) (See Section 2);
4. promote computing education research by highlighting research-led professional development and classroom resources (see Section 4a and Section 4b);
5. continue to grow initiatives that highlight computing research and support teacher engagement such as the Raspberry Pi Computing Education Seminars[19], NCCE quick reads[20], CAS research working group activity[21], UK SIGSCE journal club[22], CAS Research computing education book club[23] and CAS Research Computing Education Student Network[24] (see Section 4a and Section 4b);
6. investigate the quality of primary teachers' experience of computing in ITT and how this might be improved (see Section 5);
7. investigate computing being offered as a specialist Primary ITT route (similar to the Maths Specialist route), including placements at schools with teachers who are expert practitioners (see Section 5);
8. encourage and support Primary and Secondary ITT providers to offer early-career enhancement courses on computing. This could match with recent DfE proposals for early career enhancement[25] (see Section 5 and Section 6);
9. encourage a community of practice amongst Primary ITT providers who have an interest in computing (see Section 5)
10. encourage research in Primary and Secondary ITT (Section 5 and Section 6);
11. consider introducing a Primary Computing Teacher Scholarship program, perhaps aligned to early career specialisation. At present, the BCS Scholarship program is for secondary school teachers (see Section 5);
12. investigate a buddying system for teachers new to teaching computing to be mentored with more experienced teachers (see Section 5 and Section 6).

10. https://cphc.ac.uk/
11. https://www.bcs.org/
12. https://www.computingatschool.org.uk/
13. https://teachcomputing.org/
14. https://www.stem.org.uk/
15. https://uki-sigcse.acm.org/
16. https://www.technocamps.ac.uk/
17. https://glowconnect.org.uk/
18. https://uas.ac.uk/
19. https://www.raspberrypi.org/computing-education-research-online-seminars/
20. https://blog.teachcomputing.org/tag/quickread/
21. https://www.computingatschool.org.uk/custom_pages/142-wheretofindresearch
22. https://sigcse.cs.manchester.ac.uk/about/
23. https://www.computingatschool.org.uk/custom_pages/142-wheretofindresearch
24. https://www.computingatschool.org.uk/custom_pages/142-wheretofindresearch
25. https://www.gov.uk/government/publications/teacher-recruitment-and-retention-strategy

Introduction

This report provides a review of how schools, in the United Kingdom, currently work with universities in the teaching and learning of computing. This review was carried out between Spring 2020 and Spring 2021 by the Council of Professors and Heads of Computing (CPHC) with the Computing At School[26] (CAS) Research and Universities Working Group (R&UWG).

This review is particularly timely as computing education in schools is undergoing a radical change (Vahrenhold, Cutts & Falkner, 2019)[27]. In the UK, education is devolved to the four separate nations. In 2012, the Minister for Education in England, Michael Gove, famously declared that ICT (Information and Communication Technology) qualifications were not fit for purpose and that they would be removed from the curriculum, leaving computer science as the main digital qualification available in England. The three other nations – Scotland, Wales and Northern Ireland reacted separately. In both Wales and Northern Ireland, ICT qualifications were replaced by new qualifications in Digital Technology. In Scotland as part of the introduction of a Curriculum for Excellence, the two existing qualifications in Information Systems and Computing had already been merged into a single set of qualifications. Each of the UK nations provides support for teachers and learners in transitioning this change. Example relationships include universities developing and delivering computing outreach events to pupils and professional development courses for teachers, universities providing initial teacher training [28], schools hosting students for initial teacher training requirements, computer science course requirements which include school placements, and schools working with universities on computing education research and curriculum development projects.

To inform this report, stakeholders and their roles were identified as well as factors which influence engagement. Teachers and university representatives were surveyed and data synthesised. During this process, particular attention has been drawn to the new and potential relationship between large scale government-funded initiatives such as Technocamps[29], Glow[30] and the National Centre for Computing Education (NCCE)[31]. For further background on these initiatives and provision of computing education support for schools see Appendix A.

---

26 https://www.computingatschool.org.uk/
27 Vahrenhold, J., Cutts, Q., & Falkner, K. (2019). Schools (K–12). In S. Fincher & A. Robins (Eds.), *The Cambridge Handbook of Computing Education Research* (Cambridge Handbooks in Psychology, pp. 547-583). Cambridge: Cambridge University Press. doi:10.1017/9781108654555.019
28 The term "initial teacher training" is used in England and "initial teacher education" is used in Ireland, Wales and Scotland.
29 https://www.technocamps.ac.uk
30 https://glowconnect.org.uk/
31 https://teachcomputing.org/

This project was led by a steering group with representatives from CPHC (Professor Sally Fincher), CAS Research & Universities Working Group (Jane Waite), Glasgow University (Dr Peter Donaldson), Technocamps (Professor Faron Moller) and Stranmillis University (Dr Irene Bell). The project employed Jane Waite as researcher. The report was written by Jane Waite with Sally Fincher.

Background

Why do, and how might, universities engage with schools

Universities may engage with schools for a range of reasons.

Universities may engage with schools for Outreach, to increase the diversity, quality and number of undergraduate applications for CS and CS ITT courses

For computer science departments, this form of engagement is likely to be centrally and strategically organised and funded, perhaps by a partnership office. Examples of activities include, students visiting the university to attend a "gifted and talented" programme, providing talks to schools about university courses and running coding competitions in university. This form of engagement can be driven by university targets and may be a core element of the marketing strategy of universities. In undertaking outreach, universities raise student awareness, knowledge, skills and understanding of computer science and about their own institution. The objective is generally to increase the diversity of student intake, increase the quality of their starting point of understanding in computer science courses and drive up the number of undergraduate applications. This kind of engagement is more likely to be with geographically local schools. The frequency of engagement is likely to be yearly or sometimes termly. The number of students engaged varies dramatically between institutions, from a few dozen to hundreds. As well as impacting potential students this form of engagement can also impact teachers, if they attend an event. Success is often measured through recruitment information. Key diversity targets include to attract students from a wider range of ethnic backgrounds, those from lower income families and from all gender preferences.

Universities may engage with schools for Public Engagement, to increase general awareness about computer science

This form of engagement may be centrally and strategically organised but is often associated with specific individuals or teams in a university who want to raise awareness of their disciplinary subject area, and who may raise funding from sponsorship and grants. Examples of activities include CS4FN's[32] production of magazines about computer science, public lecture series and organising or taking part in science fairs. These activities may be less locally targeted, and are likely to be less frequent. The outcomes of public engagement, for students and teachers, are similar to outreach: increasing awareness, knowledge, skills and understanding of computer science and about the host institution. As the target audience is wider than outreach it can be hard to directly measure the impact of these initiatives, as their aim is disciplinary, their effect ripples beyond a single institution.

Universities may engage with schools for school teacher CPD, teacher support and school resource production, to improve CS provision in general.

For Computer Science departments this engagement can be classified as outreach as pupils are impacted, in terms of their awareness, knowledge, skills and understanding of Computer Science, as their teachers' expertise is increased. For education departments this engagement may be classified as "core business" as teachers' ongoing professional development may be part of the portfolio of courses provided.. This form of engagement may be centrally and strategically organised, particularly if it is associated with large programmes of work funded by the government.

[32] http://www.cs4fn.org/

Conversely these initiatives have historically been smaller scale and associated with specific individuals or teams in a university who want to raise awareness of their subject and who raise funding from sponsorship and grants. Examples of activities include Technocamps' Technoteach[33] programme and portfolio of teacher resources, Network of Excellence[34], Teaching London Computing[35], elements of the National Centre for Computing (NCCE)[36] such as Isaac Computer Science[37], supporting elements of Professional Learning and Networking for Computing (PLAN C)[38] and running local teacher training courses and developing teaching resources. These activities can be either locally targeted or wider reaching and can be regular or infrequent.

Prior to there being a requirement for computer science to be taught in schools, this form of engagement was generally minimal. As curriculum changes were introduced there has been increased demand for teacher CPD in computer science and for school resources. This demand has changed recently, influenced by the introduction of several large scale national government-funded initiatives. For example, in Wales, university involvement has increased with Technocamps. In England university involvement increased with the Network of Excellence[39] (for some universities) and is now decreasing with the Network of Excellence school centred approach of teacher CPD and support (see Appendix D). In Scotland, university involvement in the formal Computing Science curriculum increased during the development of Curriculum for Excellence and projects such as the Royal Society of Edinburgh's exemplification of Computing Science and PLAN C before returning back to focus on individual universities local priorities and needs. Outcomes for teacher CPD can be hard to measure, as can the impact of resources developed. Involvement in such initiatives can be high risk, with a high cost to universities, but the impact may also be considerable.

Universities engage with schools for finding placements for education modules in Computer Science departments

This form of engagement is where computer science departments offer modules within the curriculum, that include placements in school and subject content on teaching, such as the Undergraduate Student Ambassador Scheme[40] (several examples of these types of course are detailed in a previous CPHC report *Promoting Careers in Computing Education: Sharing Practice*[41]). As part of the core offering these are, in theory, strategically organised. However, in many universities, individuals or groups of individuals run these courses with little central support. There are associated risks; institutional reputation can be damaged if students are of poor quality. Often personal relationships are used to find schools, and if staff change, these links may not be maintained. However, the benefits to students, schools, and universities can be very high. This engagement is a high-quality method of providing outreach and public engagement and supporting the development of disciplinary improvements as close links are made with teachers who are then likely to attend CPD. However, whether the impact is being effectively measured is not clear.

33 https://www.technocamps.com/en/programmes/#section-technoteach
34 https://www.computingatschool.org.uk/custom_pages/35-noe#:~:text=The%20Network%20of%20Excellence%20(NoE,computing%20at%20the%20national%20level.
35 https://teachinglondoncomputing.org/
36 https://teachcomputing.org/
37 https://isaaccomputerscience.org/
38 https://trace.dcs.gla.ac.uk/planc/
39 https://www.computingatschool.org.uk/custom_pages/35-noe#:~:text=The%20Network%20of%20Excellence%20(NoE,computing%20at%20the%20national%20level.
40 https://uas.ac.uk/
41 https://cphcuk.files.wordpress.com/2018/08/cphc_promoting-careers_report.pdf

Universities engage with schools for finding primary and secondary placements for initial teacher training (ITT) in Education departments.

This form of engagement represents the "core business" of education departments in the initial teacher training (ITT) of secondary computing teachers and in the inclusion of computing in primary teacher training. These modules are part of the core offering, and so centrally and strategically organised. Finding suitable secondary schools can be hard. For primary placements, computing provision in schools is variable. As of 2nd February 2020, there were 580 Secondary Computing ITT courses and 1,911 Primary ITT courses listed in England on the Department for Education teacher training website[42] . Each of these courses may be run by a University or School Centred Initial Teacher Training (SCITT) route. SCITTs are required to work in close partnership with universities. However, the extent of this collaboration varies. Not all entries in the DfE list of ITT providers show an associated university. The majority of students are at university led providers. Cohorts at SCITTs can be very small. Out of the 580 potential ITT courses offered many may not recruit.

In Scotland the responsibility for sourcing and allocating school placements was centralised and is now carried out by the General Teaching Council for Scotland (GTCS). This change also involved moving to an opt-out system where schools have to provide reasons why they are unable to host student teachers. Universities, who are the sole providers of Initial Teacher Education in Scotland, share their placement requirements with the GTCS who then try to allocate students to schools within reasonable travelling distance of their main residence. Although there have been benefits from moving to a centralised approach the relationship between specific Initial Teacher Education providers and schools is weaker as students can be placed in schools anywhere in Scotland.

The level of support and mentoring available to Secondary Computing teachers on placement can also dramatically vary due to the limited number, and uneven spread, of Computing specialists within some local authorities.

Universities engage with schools for finding schools to take part in Computer Science Education Research.

Computer Science Education researchers may engage with schools, including teachers and/or students. The availability of both funding and of researchers with experience in this field is very limited. There are issues as to whether this field of research falls within the remit of computer science departments or education departments and whether universities see this as a good area to invest effort in. Research is driven by whether papers produced are judged to be high quality and can be put forward for the Research Excellence Framework (REF)[43], the system for assessing quality of research in UK universities. The number of Universities offering PhD places in Computing Education is very limited, as is the probability of finding funding to support research given the remits of different funding councils. The lack of funding deters senior management from appointing Computing Education research-focussed staff, as there is no clear path for career development.

---

42 https://find-postgraduate-teacher-training.education.gov.uk/results?l=2&subjects=48&qualifications=QtsOnly,PgdePgceWithQts,Other&fulltime=False&parttime=False&hasvacancies=True&senCourses=False
43 https://www.ref.ac.uk/

However, with recent curriculum changes, there may now be an opportunity to lobby for distinct funding to support the research of the teaching and learning of computing in schools, and of computing education in general.

Just as there are many reasons for universities to engage with schools, schools may engage with universities for a range of reasons.

Schools engage with universities for outreach activities for their pupils

Outreach can be an important way to raise pupil aspirations as well as helping pupils become aware of opportunities for further education and careers. In England, recent changes to school regulatory requirements[44] have focused attention on this area as pupils must be offered experiences with industry and further study opportunities regularly. In Scotland there is a National Developing the Young Workforce (DYW) Strategy[45] which aims to connect employers with schools in order that pupils develop a greater understanding of modern workplaces and the skills required.

Schools engage with universities for teacher continuing professional development (CPD) and support and resources

Universities can provide teachers with computer science professional development, classroom resources and local support including networking and community activity. Funding may be provided through large scale initiatives, such as Technocamps[46], NCCE[47], Teaching London Computing[48] and Data Education in Schools[49] or through small scale local contacts.

Schools engage with universities for initial teacher training and computing student school placements

Having university students in school can be an effective way to increase pupil interest in a subject and higher education. Also, schools may have this as part of their priorities or business model. They may be teaching schools or may be providers of Initial Teacher Training (School-based ITT) and need to engage with universities as partners in such programs.

---

44 https://www.gov.uk/government/publications/careers-guidance-provision-for-young-people-in-schools
45 https://www.dyw.scot/
46 https://www.technocamps.ac.uk/
47 https://teachcomputing.org/
48 https://teachinglondoncomputing.org/
49 https://dataschools.education/

Schools engage with universities for research

To improve teaching and learning, for career development and for personal interest teachers may engage with universities to take part in, and to find out about, research. Research may be translated into a format that is more accessible than the original academic output. Such translation work can be done by the original authors of research, by third parties (such as the NCCE quick reads[50]) or by teachers themselves. Some computing education research seminars, conferences, book clubs and network meetings are aimed at, or welcome, teacher participation such as Raspberry Pi Computing Education Seminars[51], NCCE quick reads[52], CAS research working group activity[53], UK SIGSCE journal club[54], CAS Research computing education book club[55] and CAS Research Computing Education Student Network[56]. But there is still much to do to engage teachers in computing education research and still much research to be done[57].

As universities and schools engage, each party sometimes acts as supplier, providing a value of some kind to the other group, sometimes as a consumer. At times the two groups work together, to achieve common goals.

For example, when a university organises outreach events, the university is a supplier and the pupils (and more broadly the schools) are consumers. The stakeholders in these relationships often extend beyond universities and schools to include third parties who organise placements or events.

As shown in Figure 1, there is a complex relationship between schools and universities. This relationship does not exist in a vacuum; other groups such as the Government, representative bodies, third party resource developers, computing education research groups and many others frame, support, take part in and influence engagement.

---

50 https://blog.teachcomputing.org/tag/quickread/
51 https://www.raspberrypi.org/computing-education-research-online-seminars/
52 https://blog.teachcomputing.org/tag/quickread/
53 https://www.computingatschool.org.uk/custom_pages/142-wheretofindresearch
54 https://sigcse.cs.manchester.ac.uk/about/
55 https://www.computingatschool.org.uk/custom_pages/142-wheretofindresearch
56 https://www.computingatschool.org.uk/custom_pages/142-wheretofindresearch
57 https://royalsociety.org/topics-policy/projects/computing-education/

Figure 1: Potential engagement activities between universities and schools.

Our Survey

Our Survey

To discover more about the landscape of the relationship between schools and universities, CPHC formed an "outreach network" headed by a steering group with representatives from CPHC (Sally Fincher), CAS Research & Universities Working Group (Jane Waite), Glasgow University (Peter Donaldson), Technocamps (Faron Moller) and Stranmillis University (Irene Bell).

In designing the survey, the Steering Group collaboratively developed the questions. The survey was designed so that each stakeholder group was asked questions which were specific to their context, responses were a mixture of Likert scale and free-text. Ethics approval for the survey was obtained, and data was handled in accordance with ethics requirements. Data was analysed using simple descriptive statistics and cross checked by the members of the Steering Group.

The survey was launched in the Spring of 2020. In late Autumn 2020 the survey was relaunched and the data spanning the two periods have been combined and are presented here. It was shared through social media, education forums, such as CAS, and through direct email to universities via CPHC. The number of respondents is fewer than our intended target, however there is particularly rich data in the free-text responses from participants which may help inform ideas and opportunities for overcoming barriers to, and celebrating benefits of, school and university engagement.

143 people completed at least one engagement section in the survey, of these 112 completed the "about you" section of the survey as well. In general respondents had a high level of confidence in teaching computing and were generally quite confident to use research to inform their teaching. More than half create resources or offer continuing professional development (CPD) for other teachers; we can view our sample as generally expert computing educators with a high degree of influence.

The stakeholder groups for which a different set of questions were asked were those working in

1. Computer science departments who run outreach which engages with schools (teachers or pupils)
2. Computer science departments who run modules which engage directly with schools, such as the Ambassador Scheme
3. Computing education researchers
4. Schools – Educators who teach computing in schools and or may create school resources or professional development on computing for others
5. Primary initial teacher training which includes computing
6. Secondary initial teacher training in computing

Questions were asked about the type of engagement between the stakeholder group and either universities or schools, whichever was pertinent and they were asked about the barriers and benefits of engagement. Details of respondent demographics can be found in Appendix B and the detail of the survey questions in Appendix C.

Section 1: CS & ITT departments who run outreach respondents

How CS departments who run outreach engage with schools

Between 14 and 17 academics responded to questions in this section of the survey.

All 14 (100%) of respondents said they taught 12 to 16 year olds in their outreach activities. Almost all also taught 17 to 18-year-olds 14 (93%) and teachers 13 (92%). Slightly fewer, 11 (78%) taught primary-aged learners.

In free-text responses to a question on the ways outreach is organised and funded, responses pointed to a wide range of circumstances in which outreach was provided. Circumstances included activities being organised by individual academics in their spare time, programmes of events coordinated by fully funded dedicated university department outreach teams and regional or nationwide events organised by external parties where academics provide specific expertise (sometimes funded and sometimes not). Specifically, Isaac Computing[58], the Royal Institution Masterclasses,[59] Lego league[60], IEEE[61], Bebras[62], Robogals[63], Museum of Science[64], a local Science Festival and Technocamps[65] were mentioned as external groups who supported outreach. These groups often provide advertising, sometimes administrative support, and in some cases, resources. One academic mentioned a UKRI funded programme contributing to some outreach for their university.

The diversity and richness of events organised by some universities were exemplified by several respondents, many of which indicated they had developed their own material for the outreach events:

> "Virtual Coding Sessions in rural Primary School via Teams using <our> own material and Hour of code material[66] – Run 6 in lockdown. Science Festival in October 2019 – Family Day Platform for Investigation Cybersecurity and AI. How are Brains learn – teaching neural networks to Key stage 2 children. Robotics – hands-on coding robots for primary schools. IEEE[67] Events." [Participant 17]

> "We are the university partner for the Bebras Challenge, and my team runs the in-person finals for it. We also run: spring and summer schools in Computer Science; RI Masterclasses[68] in Computer Science; Women in Computer Science days; CS taster sessions for visiting school groups; CS Day Schools; mother/daughter coding days; CS interviewee drop-in service… Also numerous cross-science/mathematical sciences outreach events with a computing strand." [Participant 125]

> "Computer science workshops for school students (accompanied by teachers) on campus, Isaac computer science CPD[69] and masterclass events, an annual conference for teachers." [Participant 94]

However, there seemed to be much disparity between universities in terms of how much support was provided for computing outreach from individuals working on their own in their own time to large dedicated outreach teams. For example, a participant wrote that he organised the outreach:

---

58 https://isaaccomputerscience.org/
59 https://www.rigb.org/education/masterclasses
60 https://www.firstlegoleague.org/
61 https://www.ieee.org/
62 http://www.bebras.uk/
63 https://robogals.org/
64 https://www.sciencemuseum.org.uk/see-and-do/engineer-your-future
65 https://www.technocamps.ac.uk/
66 https://hourofcode.com/uk
67 https://www.ieee.org/
68 https://www.rigb.org/education/masterclasses
69 https://isaaccomputerscience.org/

"Individual interest of one professor (me)." [Participant 20]

Whereas another commented that outreach was provided centrally:

"By the University School of Computing outreach team with a budget allocation from the School plus external funding for Isaac Computer Science[70] events, plus interest of School staff and students, plus 2 students per year on a credit-bearing students into schools module." [Participant 94]

Another mentioned providing outreach as part of a large scale government-funded program:

"Technocamps programme: based at Swansea University but with a hub in the computer science department of every (campus-based) university in Wales." [Participant 137]

Participants were asked how many times they ran school computing outreach events and how many students they reached per year.

Most, 11 (65%), ran 1 to 10 events a year, a quarter, 4 (24%), ran more than 20 events a year, 1 (6%) ran 11 to 20 events, and 1 (6%) ran Technocamps events which provide over 1000 individual activities throughout Wales each year (including around 25 in school day-long workshops each week).

In terms of student reach per year, again there were wide variations from 1 to 50 school students to over 1,200. 5 (29%) said they reached between 1 and 50 students each year, 3 (18%) 51 to 100 students, 2 (18%) 100 and 1 to 200 students, 4 (24%) 201 to 500 students a year and 3 (18%) over 501 students a year. For the 3 universities with the largest reach, 1 said they reached more than 500 students across their projects, another 600-800 per year and the third was Technocamps[71] that reached 8000 secondary students and 4000 primary students in Wales.

Teacher facing events were reported as being less frequently delivered by responding universities. The vast majority of respondents, 13 (76%) said they provided between 1 to 5 events a year to teachers, 2 (12%) said they provided 6 to 10 events. In free-text, several educators mentioned they were previously a Computing at School[72] (CAS) Regional Centre (See Appendix D) and had not delivered teacher events this year.

The change in outreach provision was explained by one academic:

"We had a larger programme of CPD running up to and when we had funding as the CAS Regional Centre. Our CPD programme has now been slimmed back to the Isaac CS[73] CPD and an annual conference. Outreach workshops for school students is running at about the same level." [Participant 94]

Another confirmed this sentiment, saying:

"A huge amount less now <as we are> no longer the CAS Regional Centre. COVID-19 has hit hard this year too." [Participant 65]

Technocamps[74] was the other larger-scale teacher provision by universities with over 150 teachers reaches in 3 cohorts of 18 day TechnoTeach teacher training. With respect to reach, over half, 10 (59%) said they reached 1 to 20 teachers a year, 2 (12%) reached 21 to 50, 2 (12%) reached 51 to 100 and 3 (18%) reached more than 100 teachers.

---

70   https://isaaccomputerscience.org/
71   https://www.technocamps.ac.uk/
72   https://www.computingatschool.org.uk/
73   https://isaaccomputerscience.org/
74   https://www.technocamps.ac.uk/

Another academic commented on how teacher continuing professional development (CPD) had reduced in length of courses but raised some benefits from online course delivery:

"For me personally the number of student events has stayed the same (1 block of 6 weekly sessions). For teacher events, it has varied. We used to do longer face to face CPD sessions with a cohort of teachers; now it's more shorter courses and one-offs. Also, mostly online (COVID-19). For our lockdown lectures which were entirely online we reached an average of 60 teachers per session, from UK and beyond – so online-ness has enabled a much greater number of teachers to be reached. Currently, I am helping on a funded program of outreach courses (some are not for teachers though) and these look to be well-subscribed." [Participant 39]

One academic commented on the different needs of schools and challenges related to running online events:

"There is an increasing demand but not enough volunteers. Rural communities do not get the same number (lack of transport, lack of ICT teachers and resources) than inner-city schools. There is a demand to do events virtually given COVID … but this requires writing new material." [Participant 17]

Benefits to engaging with schools

University outreach providers were presented with 15 potential benefits and a free-text question. For each potential benefit, they could select from a 1 to 5 Likert scale, where 1 was the most important benefit and 5, not a benefit. We have reported on scales 1 and 2 combined and 3 and 4 combined to simplify data analysis.

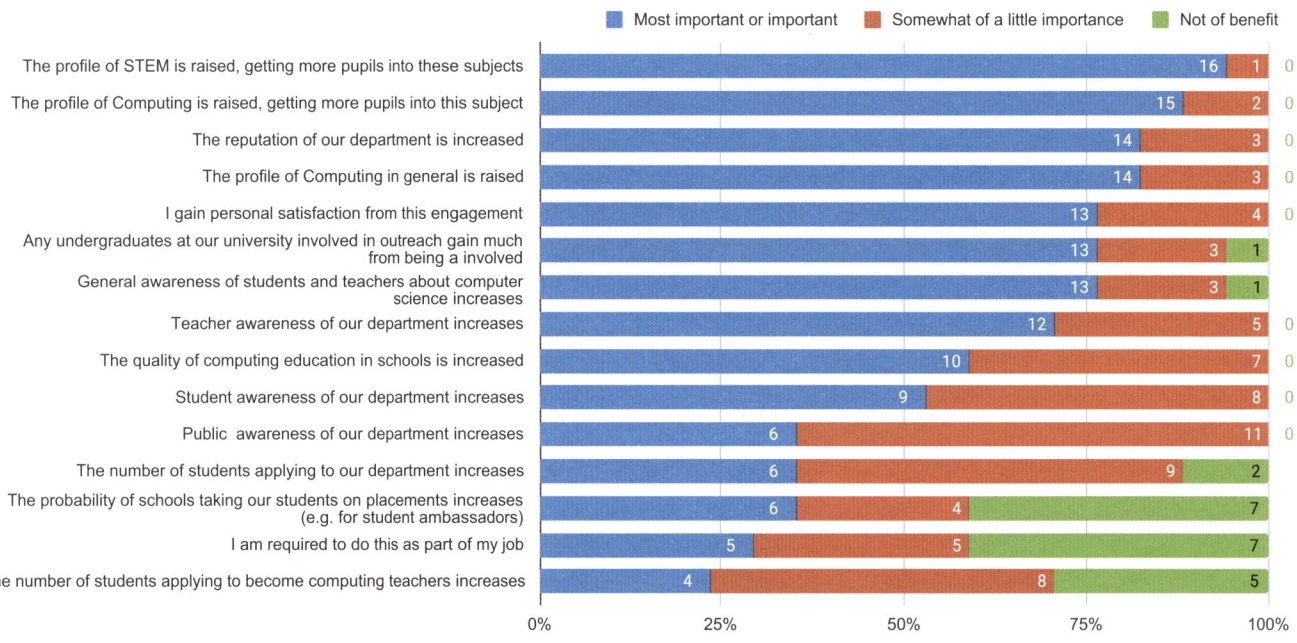

Figure 2: What are the benefits of outreach with schools for universities? (Click here for an interactive version of the chart)

As shown in Figure 2, responses fell into four bands, a high benefit, mid, low benefit and a spread of views. Within the high benefit band, there were four themes, a general increase in awareness and profile of computing and STEM, an increase in awareness and reputation of the departments organising the outreach, personal satisfaction and university students involved in outreach gaining from being involved.

16 (94%) said that raising the profile of STEM and getting more pupils in these subjects was the most important or an important benefit, 15 (88%) similarly said raising the profile of computing and getting more pupils into the subject, 14 (82%) said the same for raising the profile of computing in general and 13 (76%) said the same for increasing general awareness of teachers and students in computing.

The benefit of raising the profile of computing for specific schools was mentioned by one respondent:

> "In rural primary schools — when pupils are say less than 70 <in the school>- you are less likely to find specialist ICT teachers. The main benefit is ensuring these children in rural areas get to have the same experiences as children in inner city schools." [Participant 17]

Another mentioned the impact on diversity:

> "Diversity of computer scientists at all levels (primary school to professor!) is increased — this is increasingly the main focus of my work". [Participant 125]

With respect to raising the reputation of the department, 14 (82%) saw this as of most benefit or an important benefit. Similarly, 12 (71%) said the same for raising awareness of teachers about the department. Personal satisfaction gained from engagement was of high benefit, with 13 (76%) saying this was the most important or important benefit. A similar proportion, 13 (76%), said that the most important was that the university students involved gained much from being involved.

In the mid band, a benefit was raising the quality of computing education with 10 (59%) saying this was of most importance or an important benefit, raising student awareness about the department, with 9 (53%) and saying the same and raising public awareness about the departments with 10 (41%) saying this was somewhat important, 6 (35%) saying this was of most importance or an important benefit.

Of low benefit was that those involved were required to "do" outreach as part of their job, with 12 (71%) saying this was no benefit or of little benefit.

There was a wide spread of responses to the question on the benefit of increasing the number of students applying to the department to study computing over half, 7 (59%) said it was somewhat important. The remainder were split with 6 (35%) saying it was either the most important benefit or an important benefit and 4 (24%) saying it was either of no or little benefit.

An academic mentioned how outreach inspired school students and revealed the creativity of university computer science courses:

> "Awareness of certain platforms and what undergraduates and masters students can do is observed by the younger students and they are generally inspired by them. We usually work with games so most of the students interested are inspired by the content and creativity that computer science can offer through our university."[Participant 98]

There were varied responses to statements on the benefit of the number of students applying to become computing teachers but generally this was considered less important erring towards somewhat important. 9 (53%) said this was an important or somewhat important benefit and 7 (47%) said this was not or only a little benefit.

Participants were split in their views on the importance of schools taking students on placements; this probably reflects whether they run this type of module. 8 (47%) said it was no or little benefit and 6 (35%) said it was the most important or an important benefit, and the rest 3 (18%) said it was somewhat of a benefit.

Barriers to engaging with schools

Outreach providers were presented with 6 potential barriers to working with schools and a free-text question. For each potential barrier, they could select from a 5 point Likert scale, where 1 was the most important benefit and 5 not a benefit. We have combined 1 and 2 for one criteria and 3 and 4 for reporting on.

As shown in Figure 3, there were mixed responses to this set of questions, perhaps indicating that universities have different circumstances with respect to barriers to engaging with schools. Nearly a third 5 (29%) said this was not a barrier at all. A lack of administrative support was generally seen as somewhat of an issue, with 12 (86%) saying this was at least an annoying barrier.

One academic explained the administrative barrier:

> "It's not that there's not enough admin support, it's that the admin load is higher than it needs to be as the process is not streamlined. It's become more streamlined over the years as I'm now in a position to say, "that thing we've been doing for the last five years is happening again" and people remember so I don't have to explain from scratch. But it does involve liaising with lots of different people and departments, so is quite fiddly. As it's annual and only for ~25 people it's never going to be 'proceduralised' in the way that our official open days are, and of course being for a relatively small number of people it's still fairly manageable but it would be fantastic to have a simpler process in place. "[Participant 39]

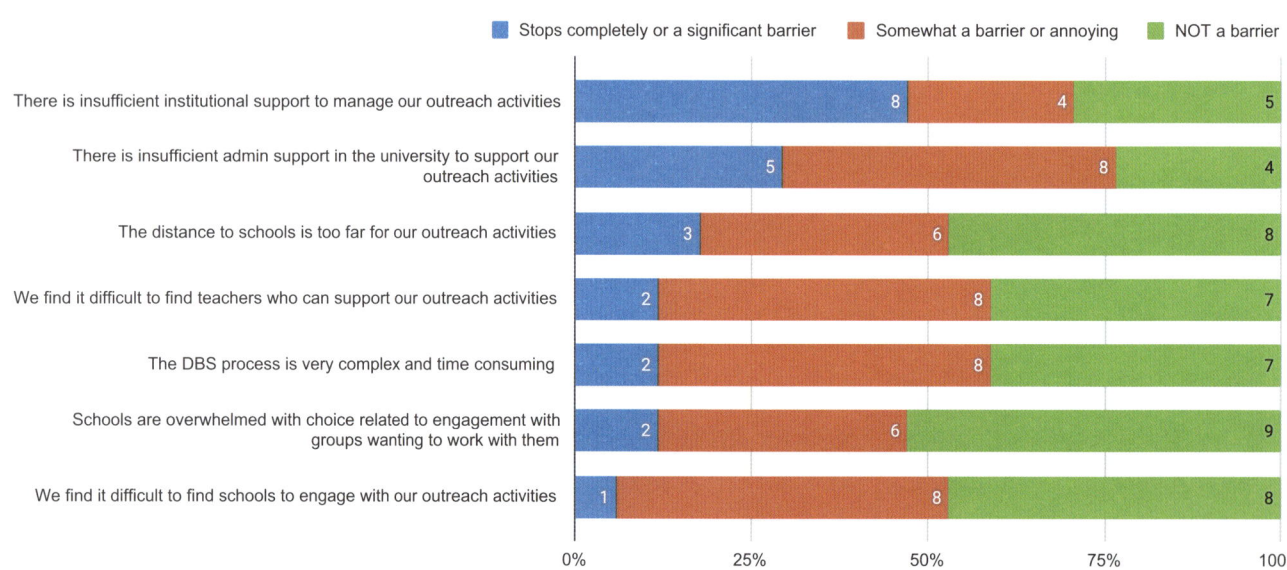

Figure 3: What are the barriers to outreach with schools for universities? (Click here for an interactive version of the chart)

Another expanded on their administrative issues as well as about finding the right schools to engage with:

> "Finding schools that want to engage with us is not a problem: finding *target* schools that want to engage is more of a problem, but not a major one. Institutional support and infrastructure is a problem for outreach in general: we have no centralised system for outreach so what technical infrastructure there is for managing outreach is varying degrees of ad hoc. Infrastructure within the department is a problem: much of our outreach is inbound and our building is highly unsuitable and far too small for running events. Our outreach is well supported by our academics, researchers and students. " [Participant 125]

All other suggested barriers were identified as not being significant by the majority of respondents. Notably, 16 (94%) reported that it was not a significant barrier to find schools to encourage to engage with outreach. Similarly, 15 (88%) said that it was not a significant barrier to finding teachers to support outreach and that schools were not overwhelmed by choice or that distance was not an issue for engagement. Obtaining DBS (Disclosure and Barring)[75] for outreach was not reported as a significant barrier by 15 (88%) of participants.

Summary of barriers and suggestions of opportunities to overcome these

There was general agreement that finding schools and teachers to take part was **not** a significant barrier, however, having institutional support for half the respondents was. This is despite significant benefits being claimed for outreach, including the increased reputation of the department, increased profile of computing and much being gained by university students involved in outreach. There are opportunities here to support the academics and staff working on outreach by raising awareness of the importance and impact of computing outreach with university management and students.

---

[75] https://www.gov.uk/government/organisations/disclosure-and-barring-service

Section 2: CS departments which run modules that engage directly with schools, such as the Ambassador Scheme respondents

The CPHC conducted a previous set of workshops focusing on careers in computing education. The report from this shared practice[76] on the structure and provision of undergraduate modules, which include school placements. These are sometimes run as part of the Undergraduate Ambassador Scheme[77], whose website gives information about the scheme for prospective schools.

[76] https://cphcuk.files.wordpress.com/2018/08/cphc_promoting-careers_report.pdf
[77] https://uas.ac.uk/

Modules with schools placements

8 university academics responded to this part of our survey. Between them they organised 10 undergraduate modules, which entail Computer Science undergraduates going into schools. Half of the modules 5 (50%) were credit-bearing and half not. Across the modules half, 5 (50%) had 1-10 students, 3 (30%) had 11-20 students, 1 (10%) module had 21-20 students and 1 (10%) 1-2 students per year.

There is little-to-no standardisation in this provision. Modules ranged from short to long courses, sometimes credit-bearing and sometimes not and with varying numbers of days in schools. Examples range from a 5-week non credit-bearing module with two sessions in school to a term-long credit-bearing course with 10 or more days in school and final year projects in schools with several months in school spread across the year. A respondent explained they sometimes organised one-off visits for students to schools who are interested in becoming teachers. The Undergraduate Ambassador Scheme was mentioned as being followed by two respondents.

An example of the type of modules offered was detailed by one respondent, one credit-bearing and one not:

> "1. Final-year 15-credit module: 10 full days in school: participating in lessons; creating and running a lunch-time computing club; assisting in an after-school activity. Assessment based on: a resourced 3-lesson plan (40%); a weekly reflective log (30%); a teacher-mentor report (30%). 2. Ambassadorship programme (voluntary): assisting in school- campus- and community-based computing workshops and clubs, and science fairs." [Participant 137]

A shorter credit-bearing course was outlined by another academic:

> "We have a 5-week module including two sessions of two hours in schools. Students generate lesson plans and reflect on the lesson afterwards." [Participant 143]

The Undergraduate Ambassador Student approach was explained by a respondent as a credit-bearing module run in his institution:

> "We broadly follow UAS: 18 x 1-hr seminars, 10 half-days / 27.5 hours in schools, acting in a range of roles from ambassador, classroom assistant, one-to-one tutor for Advanced Higher (A-level) projects, observer. Must deliver one lesson-length workshop devised by themselves, in the unplugged style. Keeps a journal during the 16 weeks of the course, and class sessions encourage critical incident analysis / reflection on events in the students' classrooms. Students write a final report capturing their learning on the course." [Participant 114]

Benefits for computer science departments who run undergraduate modules with school placements?

Participants were presented with 10 potential benefits from working with schools in this area and could select from a 5 point Likert scale from 1 to 5 (with 1 being of most benefit, and 5 not). We have grouped scales 1 and 2 together and 3 and 4 together to simplify reporting.

As shown in Figure 4, responses fell into three categories of high, mid and low benefit. In the highest benefit category, there were four themes, undergraduate student benefit, raising the profile of subjects and getting students into subjects, improving how computing is taught in schools and personal enjoyment of engaging with schools. The benefit with the highest scores was that undergraduates gain much from the placement. All 8 (100%) respondents ranking this as being of importance or of most benefit. Raising the profile of computing in general and getting more students into the subject were also seen as of high benefit, with all participants (100%) ranking these as being important or of most benefit. Raising the profile of STEM was seen as less important with 7 (87%) seeing this as important or of most benefit. Raising the quality of computing education was a third strand of the high priority, with 7 (87%) seeing this as important of the most benefit with a similar response and percentage for personal enjoyment of working with schools.

Mid importance responses fell into two themes: the first about the impact on the profile of their department and the second about school teacher recruitment. 5 (62%) said it was important or most important to engage with schools on these kinds of modules for raising the profile and reputation of their department and university. Surprisingly perhaps, only half, 4 (50%), saw increasing the number of computing teachers as important or of most benefit.

Of low importance was one item, that academics are required to organise these kinds of modules for their jobs, with 4 (50%) respondents saying this was not a benefit, 3 (37%) saying it was little or somewhat important.

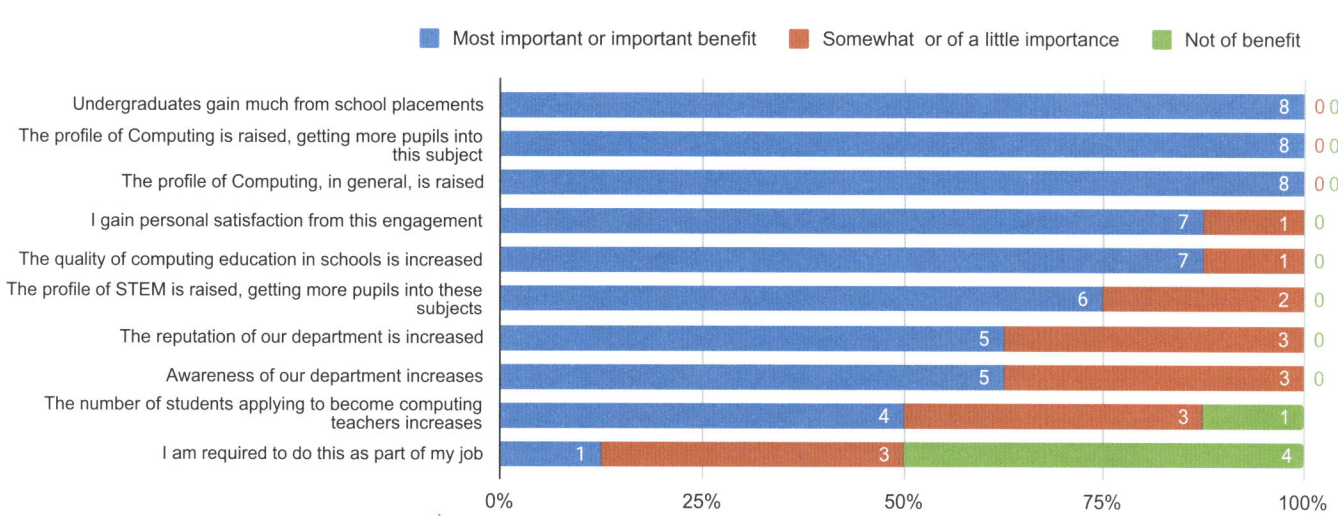

Figure 4: What are the benefits for computer science departments who run undergraduate modules with school placements? (Click here for an interactive version of the chart)

Free-text responses about benefits supported the findings of the closed questions, with emphasis on the skills students develop in terms of communication, self-confidence, agency. There was also reference to the teachers' appreciation and increased understanding the academics get of what and how computing is taught in schools. Academic 113 referenced all these aspects in his comment:

> "Everyone wins from this course. The students view it as a hobby, quite different from their other courses, and take real ownership of their work, much as some students do of their Honours project. The teachers recognise their own shortcomings in (nearly always) not having recent industry experience and so highly value having young enthusiasts who often have been in high-profile companies in their preceding summer placement or who are undertaking exciting project work. The pupils regularly are reported as asking the teacher *when's XXX coming in again?* – partly one assumes because XXX made a change, of course, but surely also because XXX was worth listening to! And finally, I, the course coordinator, learn a lot from the class sessions, the discussions for which roam freely having started from fixed points coming from the students' journal writing." [Participant 113]

This sentiment was echoed by another participant:

> "Such a module is great for developing our students' self-confidence and professional skills. It also helps us develop better relationships with our local schools and gain a better understanding of what they are teaching their students about computing." [Participant 93]

Academics believe that this kind of initiative increased student applications for their departments and smoothed the transition from school to university. An academic mentioned how more "computing savvy" school pupils were now. A third commented that they saw more of an emphasis on preparation for exams in schools.

One academic referred to how relationships between teachers and academics was important for one-to-one professional development:

> "Trust has been built over a number of years, to the point where teachers are provided opportunities to engage directly with us for crucial professional development." [Participant 138]

Barriers to engaging with schools

Universities that provide student ambassador type modules were asked about the barriers to working with schools. They were presented with 7 statements to which they could select from a Likert scale of 1 to 5, where 1 was this completely stops us to 5 this is not a barrier. Scales 1 and 2 were combined as was 3 and 4 to simplify reporting.

As shown in Figure 5, responses to barriers and issues reported by academics who organise undergraduate modules with school placements can be grouped into a set of responses calling for support and mid and low barriers. The call for support was reported in free-text, the request was for help in publicity and getting schools to engage on the student ambassador programmes. As put by an academic in response to a question on what help was needed: "Facilitate contact with schools. Get us through the front door."

Schools and universities, how do they work together to support the teaching and learning of computing?

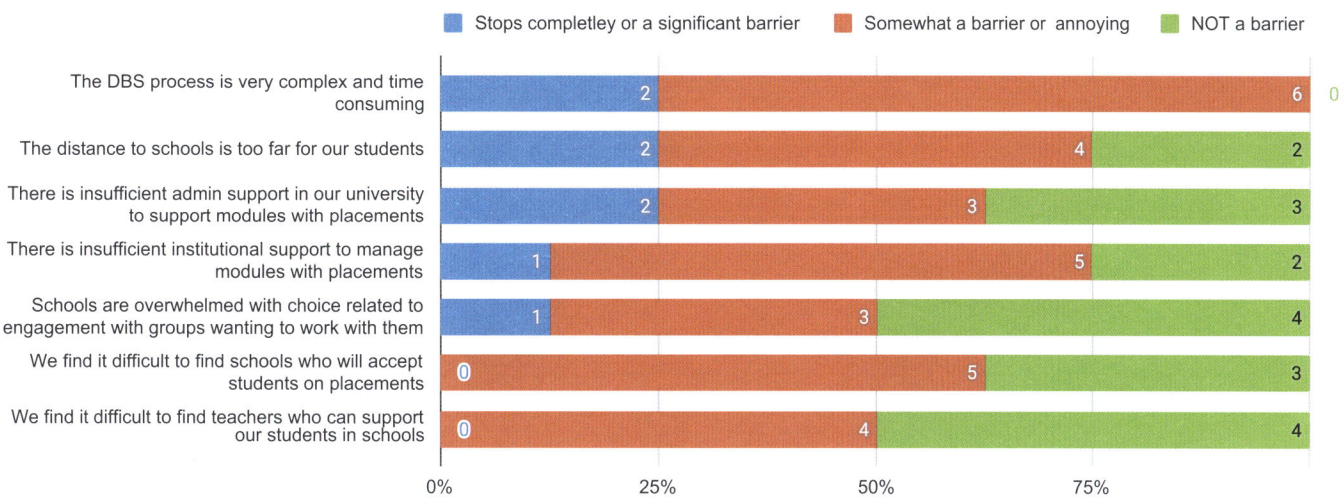

Figure 5: What are the barriers for computer science departments who organise school placement based modules in working with schools? (Click here for an interactive version of the chart)

In Likert scale responses the issue of finding placement schools was an issue and mentor teachers to support undergraduates was seen as being somewhat of a barrier by more than half 5 (62%) of respondents and it was not an issue for the other 3 (38%). More of a problem was administrative issues, such as organising DBS (Disclosure and Barring)[78] with 2 (25%) stating this was a significant issue, as was the distance of schools for students and insufficient administrative support. Academic staff often organise all aspects of placements in Computer Science departments, whereas in Initial Teacher Training (ITT) departments there are dedicated administrative staff to support this.

In comparison to universities placing ITT students in secondary schools (see Section 6), the issue of schools being overwhelmed with choice was not a barrier for Computer Science undergraduate modules. Half of the Computer Science academics who run modules with placements, 4 (50%) said finding schools was not a barrier, however, one academic reported it as a significant barrier. Local circumstances may play an important role in school recruitment.

Personal relationships built up over time with schools may also play a part in finding schools. This was explained by one academic:

> "I've mostly found it hard to get the attention of teachers via email. Once we've made contact we find that they are very enthusiastic about our placement scheme." [Participant 93]

The free-text responses identified the need to share more about the benefits of such schemes for schools, universities and undergraduates. For schools, so that they will take students, for universities so they will provide administrative support (or for placement management to be recognised as a component of academic workload) and for students, so they will take these elective modules.

---

78 https://www.gov.uk/government/organisations/disclosure-and-barring-service

One academic highlighted this issue:

> "Students sometimes don't understand the value and importance of working with schools" [Participant 61]

Another highlighted the importance of selecting the right undergraduates for this type of module:

> "Some students in the past have taken the credit-bearing module as an "easy option" and have not been the best ambassadors for the University. Careful filtering of applicants is important." [Participant 138]

Academic 143 revealed how administration was undertaken in personal time to make such courses happen:

> "The administrative process is the most challenging. We rely on academics investing personal time to make it happen." [Participant 143]

This was reiterated by another respondent:

> "better support from core and also more integration with programmes in local area schools is needed." [Participant 133]

Summary of benefits and barriers and suggestions of opportunities to overcome barriers

In summary, there are significant benefits to computer science university students taking modules which allow them to undertake placements in schools. The students, academic staff, teachers and students benefit from sharing experience from the university context to the school context and vice versa. Further benefits include raising the profile of computing as a disciplinary subject, increasing undergraduate recruitment and teacher and academic professional development opportunities. Important to all this are the personal relationships between academics and teachers.

Barriers include administrative issues within universities, often specific academics with an interest in education set up this kind of module, and they are not provided with sufficient administrative support. Distance for undergraduates to travel to schools can be an issue. What might be thought to be a significant barrier, finding placements schools, was only reported as "somewhat" of a barrier. However, in free-text responses, academics asked for more to be done to raise the profile of such schemes to help get teachers on board. Once links between universities and schools are established then longer term relationships can be fostered, and the computer science school-based modules can become an important ongoing school provision which is a win-win for all.

There is a clear opportunity to better promote the value of Computer Science undergraduate module placements in schools and perhaps to work with https://uas.ac.uk/ to advertise computing ambassador placements. It would be of benefit to universities if the profile of such schemes were raised, so that academic effort was appropriately recognised.

There is an opportunity to promote competencies in being able to teach others as a general Computer Science expertise which is useful for the IT profession more generally. For example, recent research in sharing research-informed programming pedagogy with IT professionals showed they were more likely to volunteer, and to train and support others in their workplace, following the course[79]. This type of activity could help increase the number of Computer Science undergraduates considering taking up ITT, retraining of staff in the workplace and the culture of IT departments. It would also be valuable for universities to share research-informed programming pedagogy with IT professionals, particularly those who organise programming learning and development or who work with voluntary organisations to run coding clubs.

---

[79] Jane Waite, Paul Curzon & Jo Brodie, 2021, Sharing research-informed programming pedagogy with IT Professionals. Submitted.

Section 3: Computing education researchers respondents

Computing Education Researchers

21 respondents identified themselves as computer science education researchers. They were asked questions about the institutional context for undertaking research, their roles in research, how their research was funded, how many computing education researchers there were in their institution, the topic of their research, what age group they researched with and barriers to engaging with schools.

The majority, 15 (71%), were undertaking research in the computer science department of a university. 1 was in an education department and 2 were in a dedicated computer science education department. 2 were employed in a research organisation and 1 in an educational resource company.

Respondents could select one or more research roles. Over a third of survey participants 8 (40%) reported they were a supervisor of others undertaking computing education research. A quarter, 5 (25%), said they led a computing education research group. 6 (30%) said they were PhD students. 1 respondent (5%) was a masters student, 1 (5%) was an undergraduate doing computing education research, 2(10%) were teachers undertaking research in their class.

With respect to funding of research, 9 (41%) were unfunded, 4 (18%) had funding from their institutions, 4 (18%) had funding from EPSRC, 1 (5%) had NSF funding which included multiple projects, 1 (5%) had funding from a philanthropic organisation, 1 (5%) was funded by the company they worked for, 1 (5%) had a doctoral training grant and 1 had large scale funding for several researchers and research projects from the Department for Education.

In terms of how many people were undertaking computing education research in their contexts, 8 (40%) had between 1 and 3 people, 5 (25%) had between 4 and 6, and 8 (40%) had between 7 and 15 researchers.

With regard to topics most were distinct but there were some common themes 5 (25%) respondents mentioned programming, 4 (18%) inclusion or gender, 3 (14%) AI / machine learning, 3 (14%) Cybersecurity.

One academic outlined the project areas being studied as:

> "Gender equity, Pair programming, Peer instruction, Non-formal learning, Physical computing." [Participant 76]

Another listed several topics of research:

> "Pair programming, metacognition and learning transfer, ipsative assessment, gender bias in IDEs, plagiarism prevention, math fear and teaching machine learning, collaboration in social networks and digital EDI (electronic data interchange)." [Participant 10]

One mentioned researching in a specific school phase, primary (pupils aged 5 to 11):

> "Primary school CS and programming education, including concreteness fading and tangible programming." [Participant 136]

With respect to age groups of students being studied in research projects, 3 (15%) reported researching computing education with pupils aged 4 years old or younger, 7 (35) with 5 to 11 years old, 7 (35%) with 12 to 16-year-olds, 5 (25%) with 17 to 18-year- olds, 12 (60%) with undergraduates or similar, 5 (25%) with teachers.

Barriers to engaging with schools

Researchers were asked about the barriers to engaging with schools. They were presented with 7 potential barriers and a free-text question. For the potential barriers they could select from a Likert scale from 1 to 5, where 1 was 'this stops us completely' and 5 'this is not a barrier'. We have grouped scales 1 and 2 as well as 3 and 4 to simplify reporting.

As shown in Figure 6, responses were very varied for most of the questions, indicating that researchers faced different barriers.

8 (42%) of respondents said finding schools to engage with for research was a significant barrier. However 8 (42%) said it was annoying or somewhat of a barrier but did not stop them, the remainder, 3 (16%) said it was not a barrier at all.

The same response was seen for engaging with teachers, with 8 (42%) finding teachers to engage with as either a significant barrier or that it stopped them completely. However 8 (42%) said it was annoying or somewhat of a barrier but did not stop them, the remainder, 3 (16%) said it was not a barrier at all.

Administrative support and institutional support for working with schools was marginally less of a barrier for most respondents, but was a barrier still for some. 7 (37%) said it stopped them or was a significant barrier, but the same number 7 (37%) said it was annoying or somewhat of a barrier. The DBS process was not seen as an issue for nearly half 8 (42%) but a significant issue for 5 (29%). This same pattern was seen for schools being overwhelmed with choice to engage with research 5 (29%) said it was a significant barrier but 7 (37%) said it was not a barrier at all. Distance to schools was only a significant barrier for 1 (5%) respondent, 15 (79%) said it was not a barrier or only annoying.

The free-text responses provided more information on barriers.

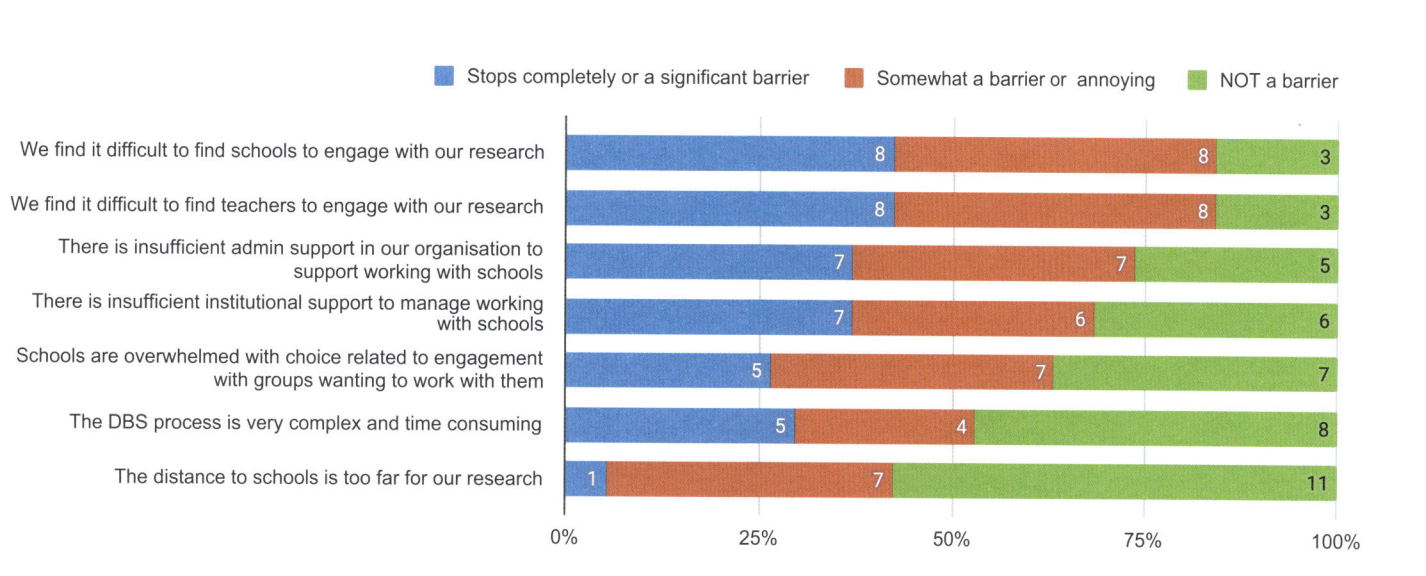

Figure 6: What are the barriers to researchers for engaging with schools on computing education research? (Click here for an interactive version of this chart)

A respondent mentioned a significant barrier that other researchers do not want to collaborate.

6 respondents said a lack of time to do research was the main barrier. Money to fund research, or lack of it was mentioned by 5 respondents, including a lack of funding for PhD students.

One researcher mentioned time and curriculum as barriers:

> "The biggest barrier we face (pre COVID) is time: time to work with teachers, and time for CS in the classroom. The second barrier we face is a lack of high quality, rigorous curricula." [Participant 35]

Several participants mentioned that teachers are so busy they don't have time to engage with research and the difficulties of fitting in with school curricula. A respondent said:

> "I suspect teacher's engagement with research is very much dictated by their workload. Also timing can be an issue if the long term scheme of work or covering of a particular topic does not fit in with the timescales imposed on the researcher." [Participant 66]

Funding and time was mentioned by one participant:

> "Lack of funding and research time, bias towards more mainstream CS research." [Participant 10]

As well as teacher time, academic time was mentioned:

> "As a Senior Lecturer (Scholarship) the only real barrier is funding to release me from teaching." [Participant 115]

A researcher suggested a national programme should be set up to fund computing education research studentships.

Participants were asked if things had changed with regard to engagement of schools with research. 4 said nothing had changed. 3 said things were worse. One commented that schools are overwhelmed and another that schools don't have time these days. 3 said things had got better, 1 referred to social media making it easier to connect with others. Another academic combined this mixed set of responses saying:

> "Yes, now schools and teachers are more interested then they were 10 years ago (since the introduction of the new curricula) but unfortunately they face more fundamental challenges and teachers are extremely busy, which can make it hard to get a response." [Participant 136]

When asked what help might be provided, one said that the profile of computer science education research needed to be raised in university settings, as it was not treated seriously at present:

> "The need to raise the status of CSE <(Computer Science Education)> and CSE research in HEI <(Higher Education Institution)> Computer Science Departments. Not treated seriously at present." [Participant 115]

Another mentioned that there was a disconnect between research and what is used or known by schools and one emphasised the importance of computer science education research:

> "It's <computing science education (CSE) research> desperately needed but the barriers are huge." [Participant 97]

Summary of barriers and suggestions of opportunities to overcome these

Lack of time and funding for research were major barriers. Other barriers seemed to be true for some and not for others. Some found it difficult to find schools to engage with and others not. The profile of computer science education research was an issue and raising its profile, including showing how it can be practically applied in schools and universities was seen as a need.

There are opportunities here to lobby for funding to support research, and to raise the profile of research in schools (and universities). Help in finding schools and teachers to take part in research could also be organised, as well as sharing success of those who have obtained EPSRC and other funding body monies with others. A centralised funded PhD scheme for computer science education could have a significant impact on research undertaken in the UK.

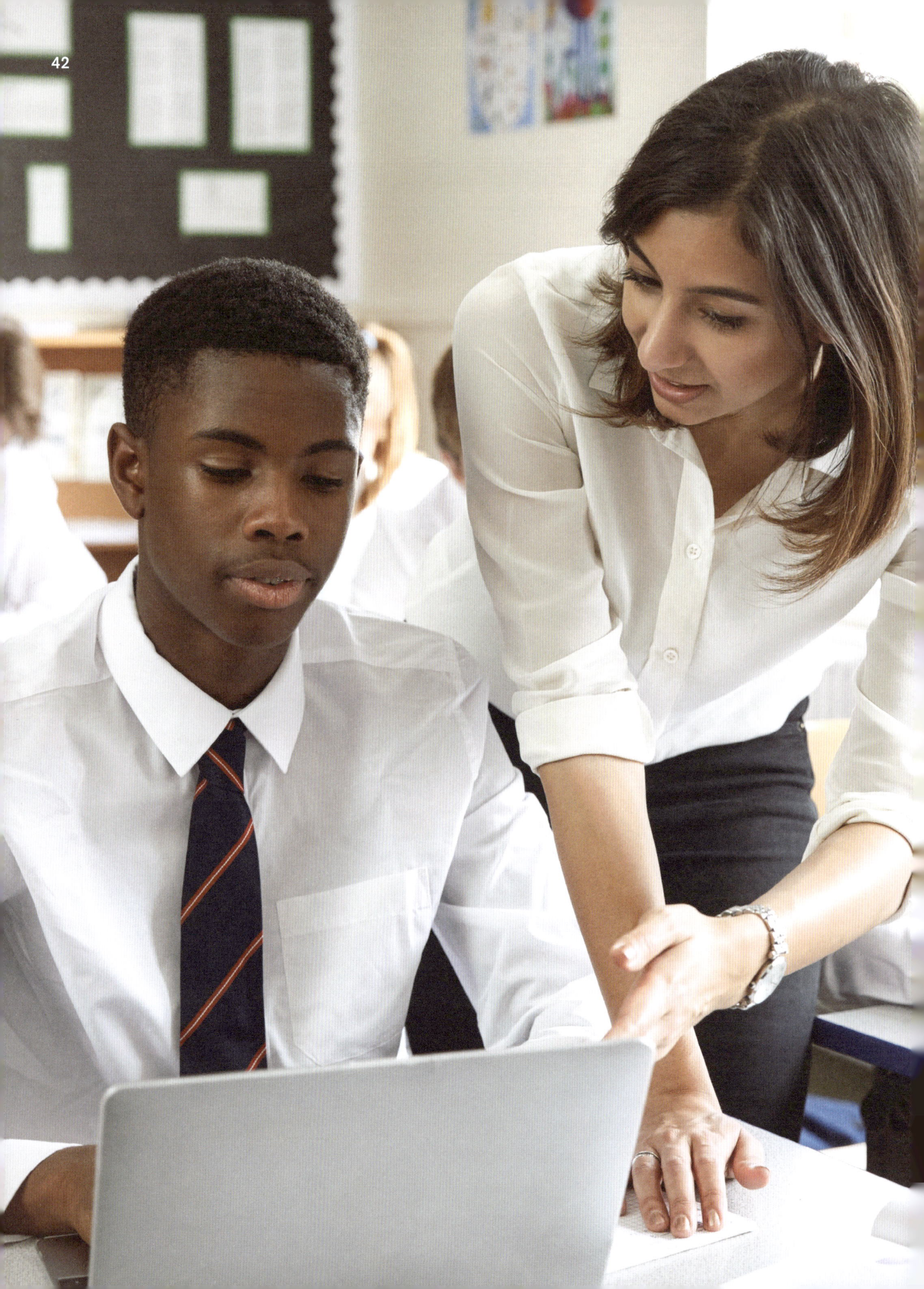

Section 4: School educator respondents

School Educators

For our survey, school respondents are teachers who teach 5 to 18 year olds in school or informal settings, educators who create resources for schools or educators who develop or deliver continuing teacher professional development (CPD) for in-service teachers. In the questions for this set of educators, respondents were asked about the context in which they taught, created resources and CPD, what their engagement with research was as well as about their engagement with universities.

In the questions on who they taught, respondents could select more than one age group. Our respondents predominantly taught in secondary schools, 16 (14%) said they taught 5-11 year olds, 44 (39%) taught 12 to 16 year olds and 37 (33%) taught 17 to 18 year olds in school.

Educators teaching in informal settings also responded to the survey with 26 (33%) saying that they taught in informal settings (such as computing clubs).

When asked if they produced resources or CPD for others, 46 (58%) of school educator respondents said they created resources and 52 (66%) said they created CPD for other teachers.

Confidence to teach computing was high with 56 (71%) saying they were either extremely or very confident to teach computing and only 5 (6%) of teachers saying they were only a little confident and no teachers were not at all confident. As well as being confident to teach computing, the respondents had quite high levels of confidence to engage with research in support of their teaching of computing with 33 (42%) reporting being either extremely or very confident, 33 (42%) being quite confident and 13 (16%) being a little or not at all confident.

Engagement with research

The school educator group was asked four sets of questions on engagement with research, the first set was on how they engaged, the second on what the benefits were, the third on what the barriers to engaging with research were and the fourth on what professional development they have had and would like on research. Between 76 and 78 respondents answered these three sets of questions.

Section 4a: How teachers engage with research

On engagement for research, there were 15 questions on different ways educators might engage with research, and an open ended question. Responses showed that some ways to engage were more popular than others. We have grouped responses into more than twice a year, less than twice a year and never.

We have used the category "more than twice a year" to establish the most common ways that teachers engage with research, as shown in Figure 7.

The most common methods were in passing, by reading Hello World or other magazines which may have research articles, with 52 (68%) doing this more than twice a year, in passing through using resources or CPD which may or may not be research informed, with 47 (62%) doing this more than twice a year. 46 (59%) found and followed people on Twitter to engage with research, 42 (54%) by looking for and using books, podcasts on computing education research and 41 (53%) by looking for and using resources that say they have been research informed, at least twice a year.

Method	More than twice a year	Less than twice a year	Never
In passing, by reading Hello World and other magazines which may have research articles	52	17	8
In passing, through using resources or CPD which may or may not be research informed	47	26	3
By finding and following research 'informed' people on twitter	46	17	15
By looking for and using books, podcasts, blogs on computing education research	42	31	5
By looking for, and using, resources that say they have been informed by research	41	29	8
By looking for, and attending, CPD which includes research elements	36	35	7
By delivering CPD that others have created which includes research	31	23	24
By finding and taking part in external research activities run by others	27	31	20
By finding and reading academic papers	25	37	16
By taking part in my own schools research activities	21	34	23
By including research in the resources and CPD I create	20	40	18
By organising my own schools research activities (please complete this survey a second time as a researcher role)	8	17	53
By writing about research in magazines and blogs	7	17	54
By developing academic research projects (please complete this survey a second time as a researcher role)	4	17	57
By publishing about research in peer-reviewed publications (please complete this survey a second time as a researcher role)	3	10	64

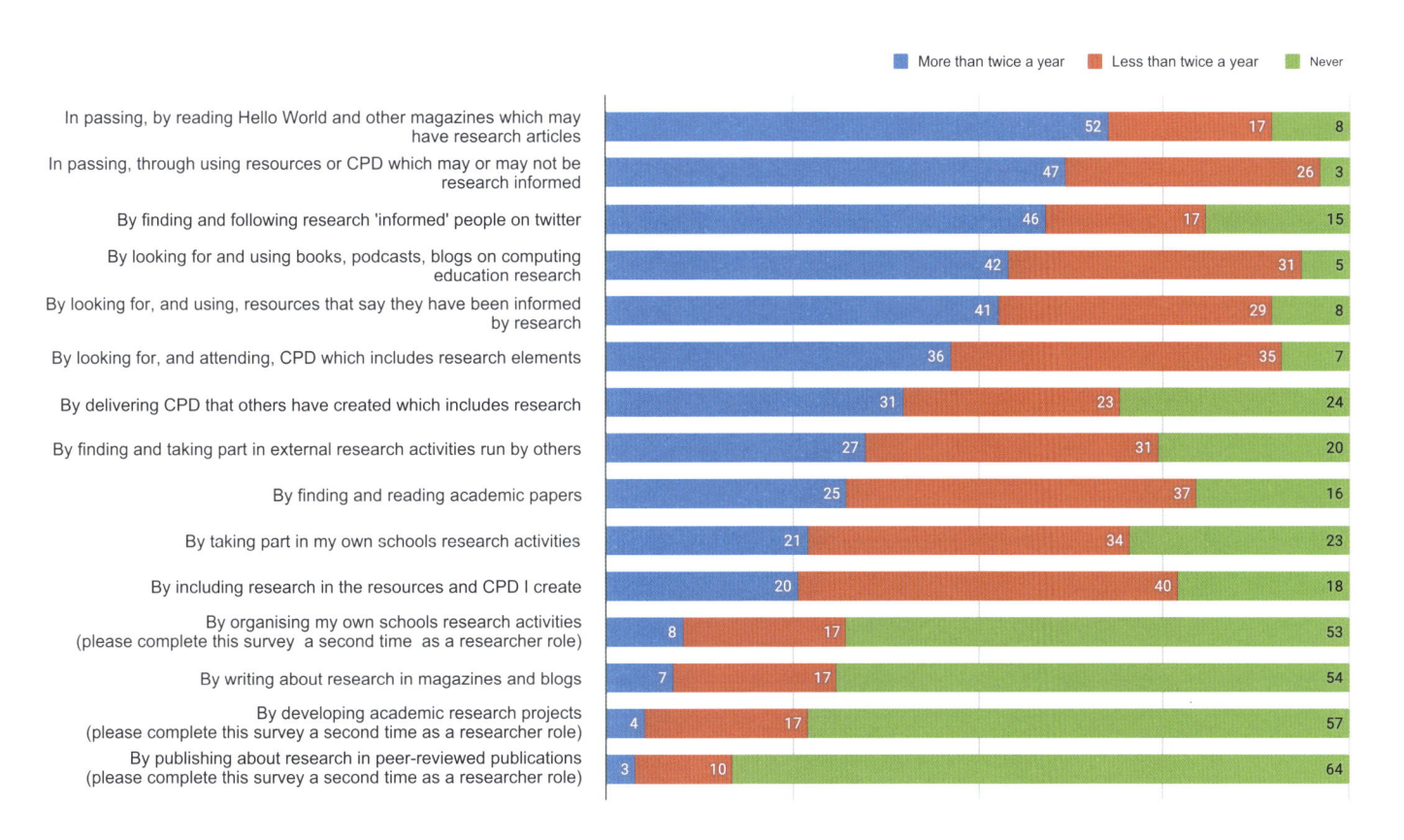

Figure 7: How teachers engage with research (Click here for an interactive version of the chart)

Marginally less popular approaches related to CPD, included 36 (46%) looking for and attending CPD which includes research elements and 31 (40%) by delivering CPD that includes research at least twice a year.

Not surprisingly the least popular approach was leading and organising research with 3 (4%) publishing about research in peer reviewed publications, 4 (5%) developing academic research, 7 (9%) writing about research in magazines and blogs and 8 (10%) organising school research. These respondents were also asked to complete the research stakeholder part of the survey.

With respect to engaging in research organised by others, 27 (35%) said they found and took part in research run by others and 21 (27%) said they took part in research in their own school at least twice a year.

Regarding finding and reading academic papers, 25 (32%) said they did this at least twice a year and 16 (21%) said never. The most important question was perhaps, whether the research was included in resources and CPD created, 20 (26%) said they did this at least twice a year, 40 (51%) once or twice a year and 18 (23%) never.

The respondents were on the whole research active in some way, only 2 (2%) said they never engaged in research in any way.

With respect to the open ended response on other ways that the educators engaged with research, Computing At School Teacher Inquiry Project[80], whilst studying for a PhD, using Facebook, professional skills development when working in IT, conferences, as a participant in research, working with researchers when developing CPD, using academia.edu[81] and taking part in the CTeach[82] programme were reported.

The CTeach[83] programme is the Chartered Teaching College's Chartered Teacher Status and includes research.

Benefits for teachers of engaging with research

The school educator respondent group was asked a series of questions on the benefits of engaging with research. In this section there were 11 questions on different ways they might benefit with engagement with research, and an open ended question. Between 76 and 78 respondents answered this set of questions. Responses showed that some benefits were more popular than others.

As shown in Figure 8 the most popular response, reported as an important or most important benefit, from 56 (74%) respondents was that their teaching was improved. The next most popular was reported by 53 (70%) of "I gain personal satisfaction" from this.

Students making more progress were reported as important or most important by 50 (66%) respondents. As an important or most important benefit from taking part in research 49 (64%) reported their enjoyment in learning about research, 48 (62%) that their confidence to teach increased and 35 (45%) reported enjoying talking about research.

---

80   https://blogs.kcl.ac.uk/cser/2016/05/09/teacher-inquiry-in-computing-education/
81   https://www.academia.edu/
82   https://chartered.college/2019/11/26/why-cteach-should-be-part-of-your-professional-development/
83   https://chartered.college/2019/11/26/why-cteach-should-be-part-of-your-professional-development/

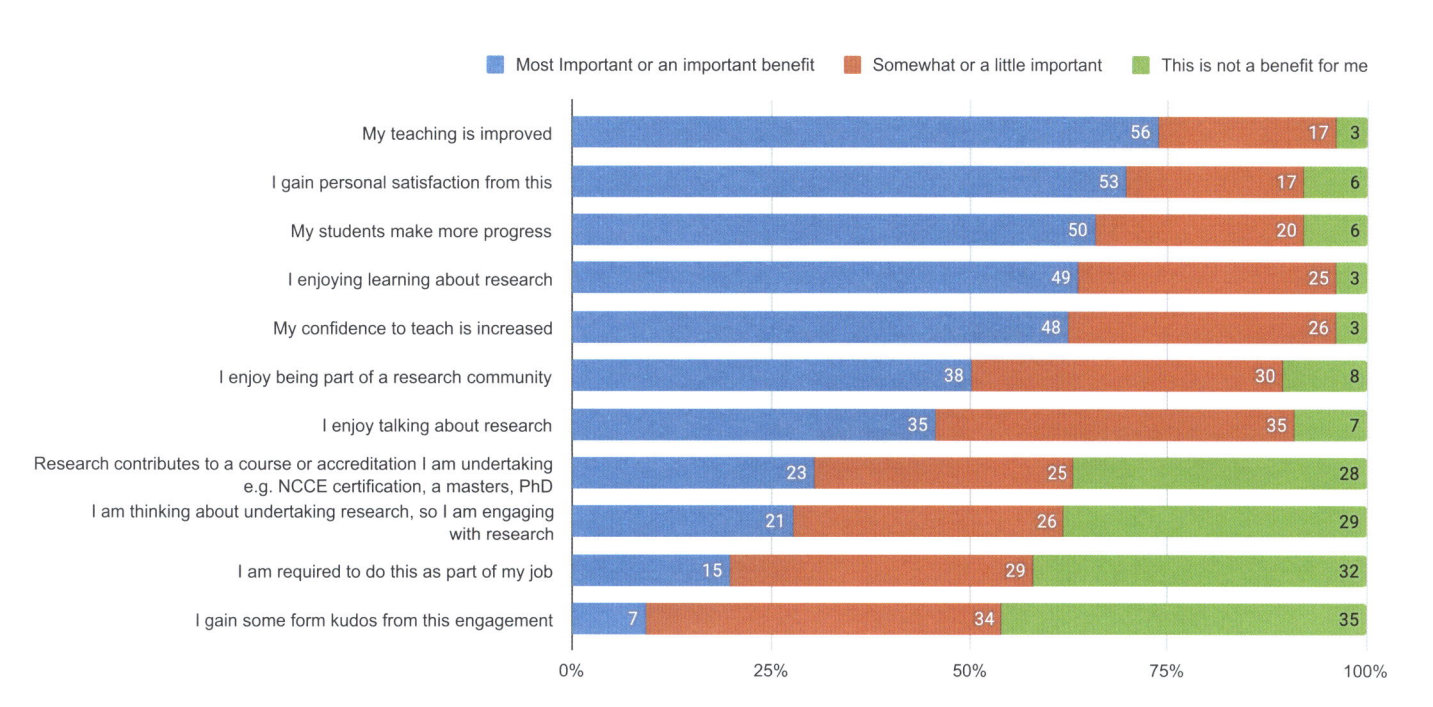

Schools and universities, how do they work together to support the teaching and learning of computing? 47

Legend: Most Important or an important benefit | Somewhat or a little important | This is not a benefit for me

Benefit	Most Important or an important benefit	Somewhat or a little important	This is not a benefit for me
My teaching is improved	56	17	3
I gain personal satisfaction from this	53	17	6
My students make more progress	50	20	6
I enjoying learning about research	49	25	3
My confidence to teach is increased	48	26	3
I enjoy being part of a research community	38	30	8
I enjoy talking about research	35	35	7
Research contributes to a course or accreditation I am undertaking e.g. NCCE certification, a masters, PhD	23	25	28
I am thinking about undertaking research, so I am engaging with research	21	26	29
I am required to do this as part of my job	15	29	32
I gain some form kudos from this engagement	7	34	35

Figure 8: What are the benefits to teachers of engaging with research? (Click here for an interactive version of the report)

Less important benefits included being required to take part in research because of external factors such as research contributing to a course or being required to do research as part of their job. 32 (42%) said research was no benefit in terms of it being required for their job and 28 (37%) said research was of NO benefit with regard to courses and accreditation.

The least important benefit was gaining kudos from engagement, with only 7 (9%) reporting this as important or the most important benefit.

In the free-text comments on benefits of engaging with research, one respondent raised the importance of confidence that other teachers could take from using resources created which were research informed saying:

> "The materials I develop for use by others can be used with confidence, as they 'go beyond anecdote'" [Participant 15]

Other comments included liking to learn new things, it being good to keep up to date, being able to have better informed discussion with other teachers as well as with older pupils and as one teacher put it to be more creative and grow in terms of teaching:

> "Ideas generate creativity and alternative approaches and help oneself grow in flexibility given so many diverse situations" [Participant 124]

Barriers to engaging with research

In this section of the survey, participants were asked 11 questions about specific potential barriers, and an open ended question on any other barriers.

As shown in Figure 9, by far the most significant barrier to engagement in research cited by respondents was a lack of time, 48 (62%) saying this was at least a significant barrier to engaging with research including 9 (11%) saying it stopped them completely and no teacher saying it was not a barrier.

Not knowing where to find research material, research material not being suitable for application to students and research not being accessible were seen as being at least somewhat of a barrier by 45 (58%), 43 (56%) and 41 (53%) of educators.

Less significant barriers were research material being too hard to understand 28 (36%) saying this was at least somewhat of a barrier, 25 (32%) saying they did not have the skills or experience to engage as somewhat of a barrier, 23 (29%) not having confidence to engage and 21 (27%) reporting their school did not support them to take part in research.

A pair of questions with somewhat conflicting responses was on how much research there was to take part in and schools being overwhelmed with choices related to groups wanting to engage with them. 35 (46%) teachers said a significant barrier to engaging with research was that there was little research to take part in, on the other hand, 27 (35%) said they were overwhelmed with groups wanting to engage with them.

The next question related to the number of professional development days allocated by their organisation across all subjects taught, compared to computing and then research. Educators were asked how many days were allocated, e.g none, half a day, one day, two days, three days, four to five days, six to ten days, more than ten days. 38 (51%) of respondents said they had no professional development on research, 19 (26%) said they had none on computing, and 8 (11%) across all subjects.

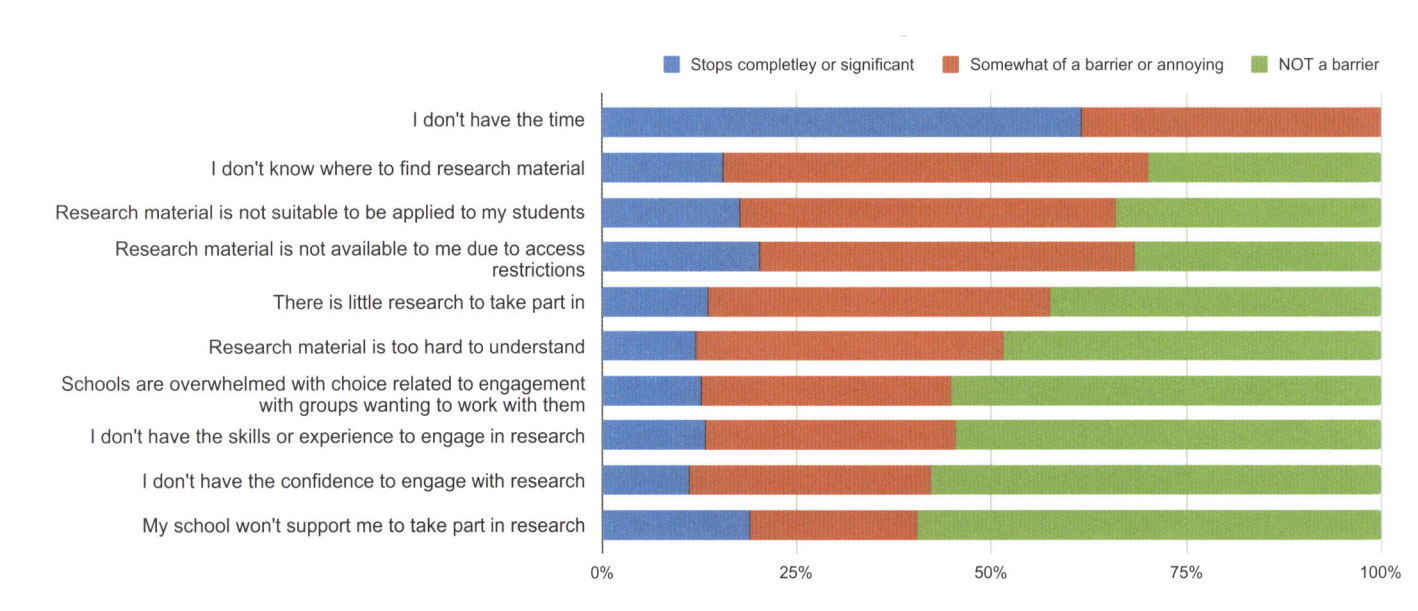

Figure 9: What are the barriers to teachers using research? (Click here for an interactive version of the chart)

About teacher professional development one respondent commented:

> "We really need to get head teachers to support teachers don't we. I suppose teachers might think of computing education research as fairly rarefied and as something that just feeds into what gets put into the curriculum, rather than something that can feed back to their own practice. Possibly we need to engage with general education platforms (magazines, websites) to get that across (as presumably it's the same for all disciplines though I've no idea if there's Biology Education Research in the same way)." [Participant 39]

In the free-text comments on barriers of engaging with research, several respondents emphasised the difficulty of finding appropriate high quality research for school contexts and the disjoint between schools and research mentioned by another.

> "The plethora of potential resources and research and the lack of any structure to find them" [Participant 42]

> "Most research is from the wrong phase (i.e. HE research to be applied in schools). Also, weakness of evidence sometimes causes concern when recommending to others." [Participant 15]

> "Research is most accessible from books on teaching computing in the bibliography at the back, but the research itself is so laborious and academically driven – a subjunct to the school system (the composite problem) itself." [Participant 124]

The COVID-19 pandemic was mentioned by several respondents as being a barrier, and one teacher made an important point that they were the only computing teacher in their school. Time, and resources being behind a paywall were repeated by several.

> "There is often not enough time to spend finding research, and this is exacerbated by the lack of access not being in a higher education institution. Also the area I am particularly interested in (computing and SEND) has limited coverage." [Participant 45]

A comment was made about the lack of A level research opportunities:

> "I haven't ever had any support or encouragement in terms of carrying out my own research and I wish but I can't afford to undertake a Masters course. No one ever approached us to be involved in any research – it almost always tends to be Secondary school focused rather than at a Sixth Form Level." [Participant 51]

An important point was raised about how research used to be cascaded before local authority control of schools was removed:

> "Having to search for your own research and CPD related to the computing curriculum. Research used to be cascaded down from universities via the DfE by local authorities. You were advised well in advance of the content of the research and CPD sessions and were able to arrange to be released from teaching to attend. This no longer occurs due to local authority budget cuts and schools becoming academies – they only provide this for the core subjects of English and Maths. Cost implications are also a barrier as my courses are approx £220 each. Schools no longer have the budget to PAY for this and pay for a supply teacher to cover your class." [Participant 80]

Several teachers raised the barrier that even after engaging with research, teachers' hands are tied in terms of teaching and learning:

> "It often seems that the deeply, deeply flawed target grades are all SLT care about, and they have entrenched, preconceived, poorly-informed ideas about what we can be seen to be doing about meeting those targets. I could be 100% up to date on research, but management has already made the decisions without consulting me." [Participant 84]

In opposition to this one teacher put:

> "I simply have no interest whatsoever in engaging with educational research as I see the research as irrelevant to my teaching." [Participant 122]

One respondent raised that a significant barrier was the lack of funding for education research.

An example of a useful approach to making research more accessible was mentioned by one educator

> "Many papers are behind a paywall which I don't have access to. Many papers contain a small amount of brilliant material wrapped up with academic language that makes them appear self important and a bit disconnected from classroom practice. I really like the NCCE quick reads as they strip out the waffle and apply the research to the classroom. I wish that there was more opportunity, time and funding for practising teachers to contribute to research" [Participant 58]

Another commented on how things have changed over time:

> "Access has definitely improved with the work of the NCCE and the CAS research working group – this has made a huge difference in terms of the profile and the ease of access for teachers (both in terms of finding research and the way it is presented)." [Participant 45]

And one commented on recent initiatives:

> "I've really appreciated the Computer Science book club and facebook research group because it's both an incentive to get involved and a supportive community to discuss ideas with." [Participant 58]

One teacher commented that it was a change in their own confidence that had resulted in a change in engagement with research:

> "For me, I have become more confident searching for open-access research online and even going to university libraries during the school holidays. That is a change in me rather than a change in the educational environment." [Participant 84].

Summary of barriers and suggestions of opportunities to overcome these

Drawing the responses together from the sections on engagement with research.

Respondents to our survey are predominantly secondary educators. In general they had a high level of confidence to teach computing and were generally quite confident to use research to inform their teaching. With more than half of them creating resources or CPD for other teachers we can view our sample as being generally expert teachers with a high degree of influence.

The school based respondents were on the whole research active in some way, only 2 (2%) said they never engaged in research anyway. Most research engagement was by encountering research in passing through it being included in resources, CPD or magazines. Some educators looked for research through following others on twitter, looking for books, podcasts and blogs. Some also took part in research led by others and much fewer were organising their own research.

With respect to the benefits of engaging with research, improved teaching, personal satisfaction, enjoyment, increased confidence and student progress were the highest cited reasons. Surprisingly engagement in research as part of courses and accreditation and as part of their job, was reported as of low importance.This is despite, research being an important part of teacher professional requirements. If this is the case for our research active, expert educators, what might the situation be for less engaged educators.

By far the most significant barrier to engagement in research cited by respondents was a lack of time. Also not knowing where to find research material, research material not being suitable for application for students and research not being accessible was seen as being at least somewhat of a barrier by nearly half of respondents.

However, recent initiatives such as the NCCE quick reads, theCAS research working group, Computer Science book club and CAS research facebook group have started to improve things.

About professional development on research

Educators were asked about the number of days of professional development they had in general, on computing and on research. They were also asked free-text response questions on what professional development on research they had had and what they would like.

Comparing the number of days of professional development allocated across all subjects, to computing and to research over half of respondents said they had no professional development time allocated for research compared to over half having at least one day on computing and two days on other subjects in general.

Just under half, 35 (47%) of respondents said they had had no professional development on research. Other responses included learning about research through doing action research, during their degree, Masters or PhD. Some mentioned learning by taking part in research projects, or attending specific courses which included research (e.g. Isaac Computing, conferences), attending Raspberry Pi research seminars, CAS research meetings and others that they were learning about research through school activity.

One exemplified how they were attending events and learning how to be a research lead:

> "Attended raspberry pi seminars, King's College research symposium, plus training as research lead from the Huntington Research school." [Participant 45]

Another commented how research was embedded in school activities:

> "Regular school-wide CPD on research + regular emails on new research papers." [Participant 117]

In responses to the question on what research CPD is needed, teachers mentioned generally how to start working with research, where to find research, professional development on how to be involved in research, how to do action research including on methodology and statistics. Mention was made about having professional development on research on specific topics, e.g. pedagogy, teaching physical computing, teaching A level students, impact of techniques, making Computer Science enjoyable.

One teacher mentioned the Chartered Teaching College's magazine:

> "Like the condensed versions that come with Impact magazine from CCT – so opportunities to discuss and apply might be good." [Participant 46]

Another suggested that research specific training should be provided including how to adapt this to the classroom:

> "Focused training on relevant research projects that would fit into the syllabuses." [Participant 110]

Another said:

> "I would love to know how to go about it properly, where I could access good resources to support me, what I would do with it etc." [Participant 51]

However, another made it clear that time was a constraint:

> "I don't think this would make any difference. I don't have the time or energy to do formal research. I barely have the time for professional reflection on my practice." [Participant 84]

About the relationship between teachers and research

Teachers were asked if they were considering undertaking computer science education research in the future. 56 teachers responded to the question, just less than half, 23 (45%), said no. Just less than a third 16 (29%), responded to say they were considering doing non-qualification based research (classroom research). 9 (16%), said they were considering a certification based qualification such as classroom research for a BCS certificate. 10 (18%) said they were considering a masters or PhD in computing education research. This means that just over half of respondents, 31 (55%), were planning on being research active.

Section 4b: How teachers engage with universities

The school educator group was asked three sets of questions on engagement with universities, the first set was on how they engaged, the second on what the benefits were and the third on what the barriers to engaging with universities were. Between 57 and 59 respondents answered these three sets of questions.

On engagement for universities, there were 8 questions on different ways schools might engage with universities, and an open ended question. Responses showed that some ways to engage were more popular than others.

As shown in Figure 10, few, only 13 (23%), of the respondents worked in schools that took primary initial teacher training (ITT) students, a similar number, 16 (28%), took computing undergraduates on placements (e.g. Student Ambassadors), more 25 (44%) took Secondary ITT students.

	At all	Never
We take primary initial teacher training students at my school	13	44
We take secondary computing initial teacher training students at my school	25	32
We take computing undergraduates at my school for placements (e.g. Student Ambassadors)	16	42
Students from my school attend university events	42	16
We use material created by universities in our teaching (e.g. posters, magazines, lesson plan materials)	38	20
I attend community events at my university	30	29
University staff deliver events at my school	25	33

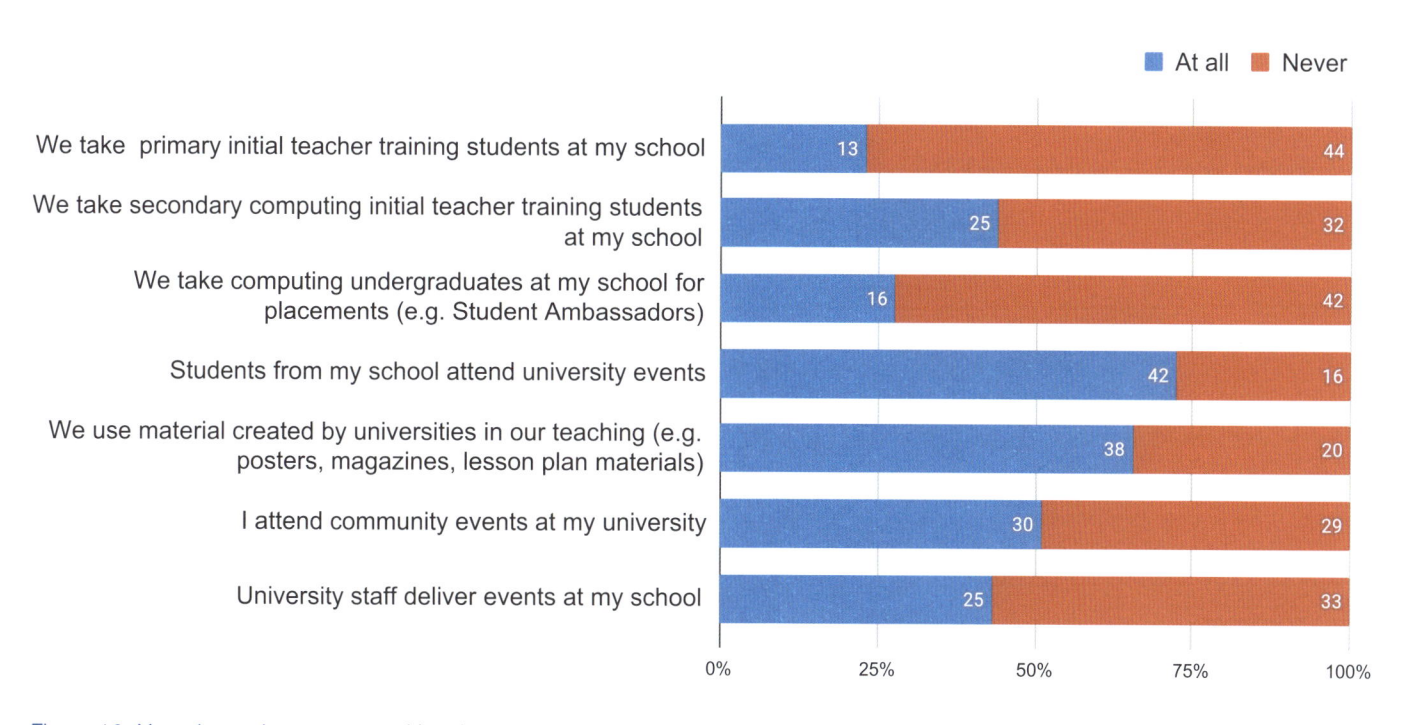

Figure 10: How do teachers engage with universities? (Click here for an interactive version of the chart)

Participants reported more engagement with universities by school students, with 42 (72%) saying their students attended university events and 38 (66%) reporting they used university created materials in their teaching (such as posters, magazines, lesson plan materials). In terms of university staff delivering events in school, 25 (43%), said this had occurred in their school.

However, there was less personal engagement by teachers with universities, with 24 (41%) saying they had attended professional development at university events and slightly more, 30 (51%) saying they had attended community events at their university.

In the free-text response on other ways that schools engage with universities, teachers mentioned careers, strategic discussions and informal discussions with personal contacts, through outreach, borrowing resources and specific programmes such as Technocamps. They also mentioned the importance of matching outreach to the right students and the difficulty of getting initial teacher training (ITT) students organised for their school.

One teacher referenced engagement of specific year groups through Technocamps:

"Technocamps programs where the team came into school to work with GCSE Computer Science groups and a year 8 group for a series of lessons." [Participant 110]

Another teacher pointed out that the outreach needs to be matched to students requirements:

"Universities do outreach days. The past experience was for middle school students and it was wasted on them. It would have been more suitable for sixth formers who would have benefited from the exposure and information and degree of expertise of the university representatives (i.e. as role models)." [Participant 124]

Not all teachers were able to engage with universities, as indicated by one teacher:

"There seems to be little on offer in our area. I would love to have ITT placement students but we are never approached, even when we have reached out. Perhaps because we are Sixth Form only?" [Participant 51]

Benefits to engaging with universities

The survey asked participants what the benefits of engaging with universities were and provided a set of suggested reasons to which they could respond using a Likert scale from 1 to 5, with one being the most positive response and 5 the most negative. 1 was "This is a most important benefit" and 5 "This is not a benefit for me". They were also provided with a free-text response to capture any other benefits not mentioned.

As shown in Figure 11, responses to this set of questions fell into three broad categories, with one set of reasons having around 70% of the participants saying they were important, the second set having around half the respondents saying there were important, and the third set with less than 20% say they were important, giving a high, mid and low banding.

The most important benefit for schools of engaging with universities on computer science was to raise profile of computing 40 (71%) said this was most important or important), and encouraging more pupils into computing 39 (69%) said this was most important or important) and similarly raising the profile of STEM in general and getting more 38 (68%) said this was important.

The least important benefits were related to kudos, being required to engage because of work expectations, planned research, or accreditation. For each of these benefits, 42 (76%), 42 (76%), 39 (71%) and 34 (61%) respectively said they were of no or little benefit.

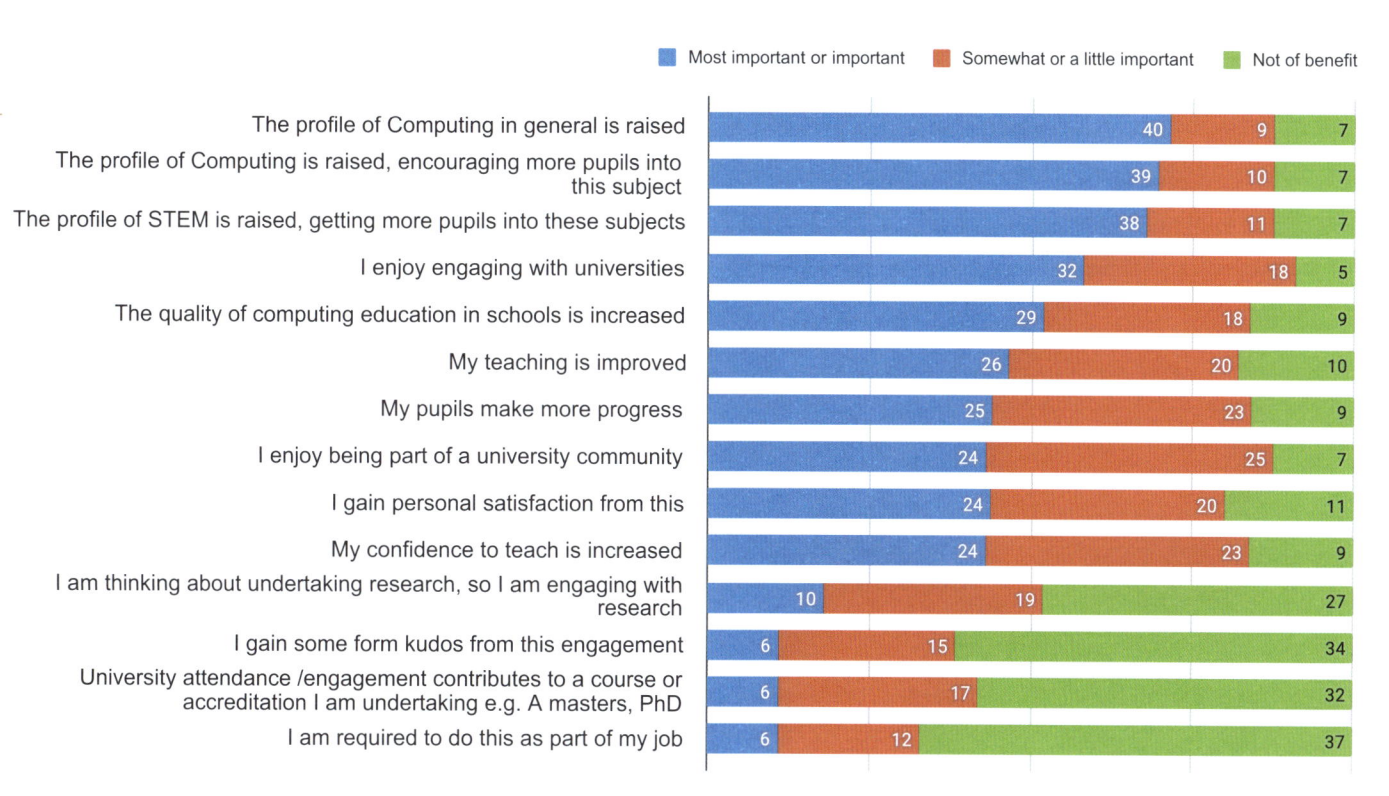

Schools and universities, how do they work together to support the teaching and learning of computing?

Benefit	Most important or important	Somewhat or a little important	Not of benefit
The profile of Computing in general is raised	40	9	7
The profile of Computing is raised, encouraging more pupils into this subject	39	10	7
The profile of STEM is raised, getting more pupils into these subjects	38	11	7
I enjoy engaging with universities	32	18	5
The quality of computing education in schools is increased	29	18	9
My teaching is improved	26	20	10
My pupils make more progress	25	23	9
I enjoy being part of a university community	24	25	7
I gain personal satisfaction from this	24	20	11
My confidence to teach is increased	24	23	9
I am thinking about undertaking research, so I am engaging with research	10	19	27
I gain some form kudos from this engagement	6	15	34
University attendance /engagement contributes to a course or accreditation I am undertaking e.g. A masters, PhD	6	17	32
I am required to do this as part of my job	6	12	37

Figure 11: What are the benefits of working with universities for schools? (Click here for an interactive version of the chart)

Of mid importance were three broad categories, the first was related to enjoying and gaining satisfaction by engagement, the second related to improvements in teaching and teacher confidence, and the third on quality of computing education and pupil progress.

Enjoyment of working with universities was cited as being an important benefit by over half of respondents, 32 (58%). Slightly fewer, just less than half said they gained personal satisfaction, 24 (43%), and enjoyed being part of a university community 24 (43%).

Just less than half, 26 (46%), reported that an important benefit was their teaching was improved, and a similar number, 24 (43%), that they were more confident because of engagement.

As well as improving their own teaching, an important point was raised in the free-text regarding by one teacher on the impact on professional development and an opportunity to highlight that CPD which is research-informed:

> "It informs the CPD I deliver to other teachers and advice on effective pedagogy."
> [Participant 45]

Just over half, 29 (52%) said that engagement was important as the quality of computing education in schools would be increased, and just less than half, 25 (44%) said that an important benefit was that their pupils would make more progress.

In open-ended responses 4 teachers mentioned that engaging with universities for students helped them have a better understanding of careers and their options. One teacher also mentioned the opportunity to network with teachers who are also interacting with universities and another that they were not sure, as their local university did not engage with them.

It seems that for those teachers who had managed to connect with their local universities, raising the profile of the subject was the most important benefit, improving teaching and learning (and professional development created) and personal enjoyment was important for around half, but there was no or little benefit for most with respect to engaging for accreditation.

Barriers to engaging with universities

Participants were asked what the barriers were for engaging with universities, they were given 7 possible reasons and an open ended response. For each reason they could select from a Likert scale of 1 to 5, with 1 the most important barrier and 5 the least, 1 "This stops me completely" to 5 "This is not a barrier".

As shown in Figure 12, responses to this set of statements can be grouped into two categories, a high level barrier and low level barrier.

The barrier which was cited by just over 50%, 32 (54%) of teachers as being significant or stopping them completely was a lack of time. Just less than half said there were no opportunities for engagement, they did not know who to contact or what universities could do for them, with scores of 26 (45%), 26 (44%) and 24 (41%) respectively.

Teachers were very unlikely to say being overwhelmed with choice for engagement was a barrier, nor that the provision was not suitable or that the universities were too far away, no teachers said this stopped them completely or was a significant barrier.

In open-ended responses, the issue of getting students off timetable, and teachers not having time to organise university visits was reiterated as well as not knowing what universities could provide and if it was suitable. Two interesting points were made, firstly one teacher explained his contact university was not his local university. He said:

> "Southampton Uni is not my 'local' university. The reason I interact with them is because of CAS. My closest university would be Oxford and I'm not confident they would even want to interact with my state school." [Participant 84]

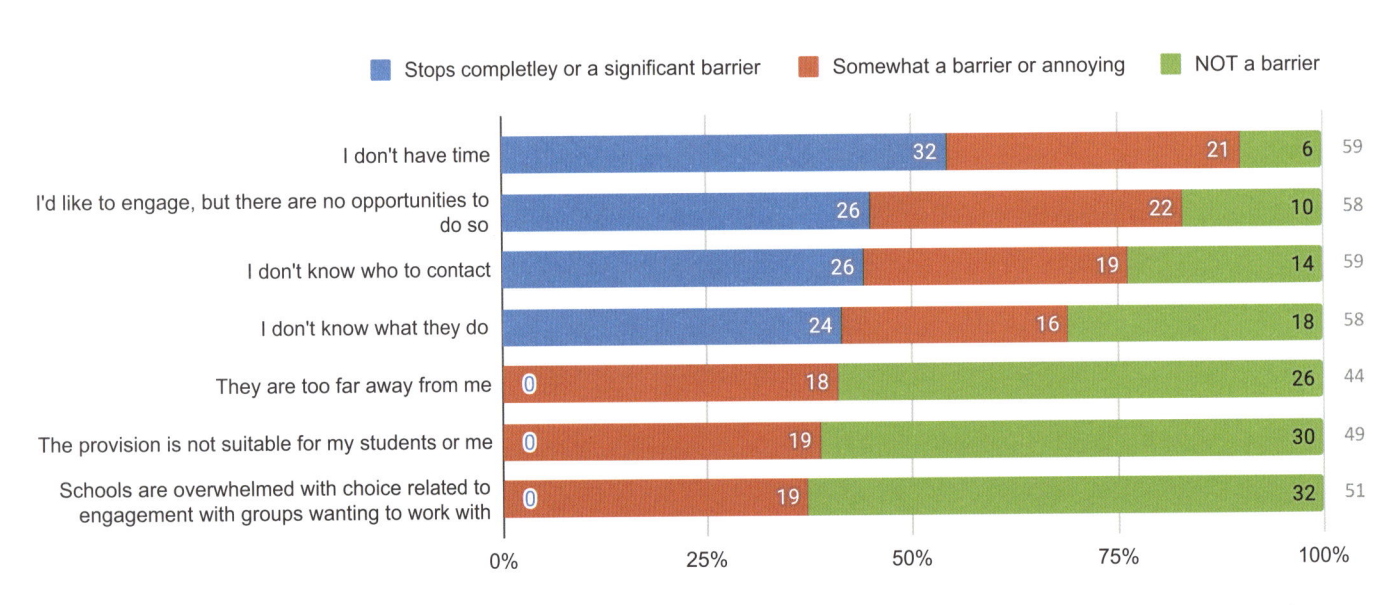

Figure 12: What are the barriers to engaging with universities for schools? (Click here for an interactive version of the chart)

Another said that he had good experiences with universities and that their university came out to his school and they were excellent. He also suggested online courses should be provided by universities for teacher professional development. A third issue raised was a frustration about whether universities valued A level CS. The teacher said:

> "I wish Universities would work with schools to understand and celebrate the value of A level CS. Many undergraduate courses repeat the content in the first year and students are actively told not to study the A level. It's very frustrating." [Participant 58]

Teachers were asked if the barriers to engaging with universities had changed over time. There were conflicting responses. 4 teachers said there were more barriers now than in the past and two said there were less.

Several reflected on changes in funding related to schools and universities as exemplified in these three teacher's quotes:

> "When CAS Network of Excellence[84] ended, opportunities to engage with universities alongside teachers decreased – the already weak bond between HE and schools was weakened further." [Participant 15]

> "Yes – previously my students visited two local universities to engage in workshops. Funding for this has been reduced so have the opportunities. Communication between university and school has declined so it's difficult to find out what future opportunities are available." [Participant 80]

> "CAS funding was stopped which got rid of the university networks. They were replaced with regional hubs in schools, so my interaction with Southampton Uni has effectively stopped." [Participant 84]

Significant barriers for around half of the teachers were a lack of time, and not knowing who to contact or what engagement opportunities there were at universities. Distance to unveristities was not seen as a significant barrier. One teacher reported getting around barriers to engaging with universities by working with a university which was not local to him, through contacts, using personal relationships, for example, through Computing at School[85]. Another teacher reported that their university came out to their school. A change in the way that funding is provided to support Computing At School was mentioned by several teachers, who explained that their link with universities had declined as a result of the change.

A significant issue raised with the relationship between schools and university was universities not valuing school Computer Science and requiring undergraduates to repeat the A level syllabus in the undergraduate year, and students being actively told NOT to do A level.

---

[84] https://www.computingatschool.org.uk/custom_pages/35-noe#:~:text=The%20Network%20of%20Excellence%20(NoE,computing%20at%20the%20national%20level.

[85] https://www.computingatschool.org.uk/

Summary of benefits and barriers and suggestions of opportunities to overcome these

With respect to taking university students on placements at school, less than half, 25 (44%), took secondary initial teacher training (ITT) students, just over a quarter took undergraduates for placements from computer science departments, such as student ambassadors, 16 (27%), and fewer still too Primary ITT students, 13 (23%). It is likely that our sample is not representative of all schools, it is likely that fewer students are taken on placements from computer science departments than was seen here. We suspect that our respondents were more engaged with universities than is the norm.

ITT providers reported that they find it difficult to find schools with mentors who could support trainees in this subject and that provision in schools is very varied. There is though in schools an ever increasing group of expert computing teachers, whether these teachers are being best used to share their knowledge with trainee teachers is not clear.

The focus for Primary ITT is not on computing, and the university-led provision on the subject was very variable. There appears to be an opportunity here to support either providers or ITT students separately with computing professional development. However, new teachers have much to learn and their time is already overcommitted. Therefore, as an alternative, continuing professional development could be used to increase computing expertise. Follow on training, perhaps as an early career enhancement courses (say at 2 or 3 years into a career) in computing subject knowledge and pedagogy could be developed in line with recent DfE early career reforms[86]. A BCS Scholarship program could therefore engage with early teachers, rather trainees. There are opportunities within such an offer to include research-informed pedagogy possibly within an action-research context which could be attractive as general professional development useful in other subjects.

For Secondary ITT, the picture is very different from Primary ITT with regard to coverage of computing subject knowledge and pedagogy. In Secondary, as specialists, computing teachers are provided with an intense training experience including action-research type activities and research informed pedagogy. However, as with Primary ITT there are difficulties with regard to finding placements. Whether any schools who offer computer science and could provide placements but are not doing so needs to be investigated. However, it seems likely that ITT providers have already exhausted all potential placements as they have local knowledge and an urgency to resolve this matter. A significant issue even when trainees are placed is mentorship. There may be an opportunity here for mentoring both trainees and early teachers to be paired with more experienced secondary teachers. However, such a scheme would need funding and careful design as in-service teachers are likely to be overcommitted in terms of teaching load.

Through engaging with universities, teachers are able to improve their teaching. However, due to changes in the funding of support for computing education in England there has been a decline in engagement between some universities and their local teacher community. How this issue is addressed is an open question.

Educators who create computing resources and professional development who engage with universities reported an increase in the quality of the material they produce because of that engagement, including the material being seen to be research-informed. There are opportunities to increase this kind of collaboration and to highlight such material to teachers.

How universities do or do not value school qualifications in computer science, and what the impact is of this, should be investigated.

86 https://www.gov.uk/government/collections/early-career-framework-reforms

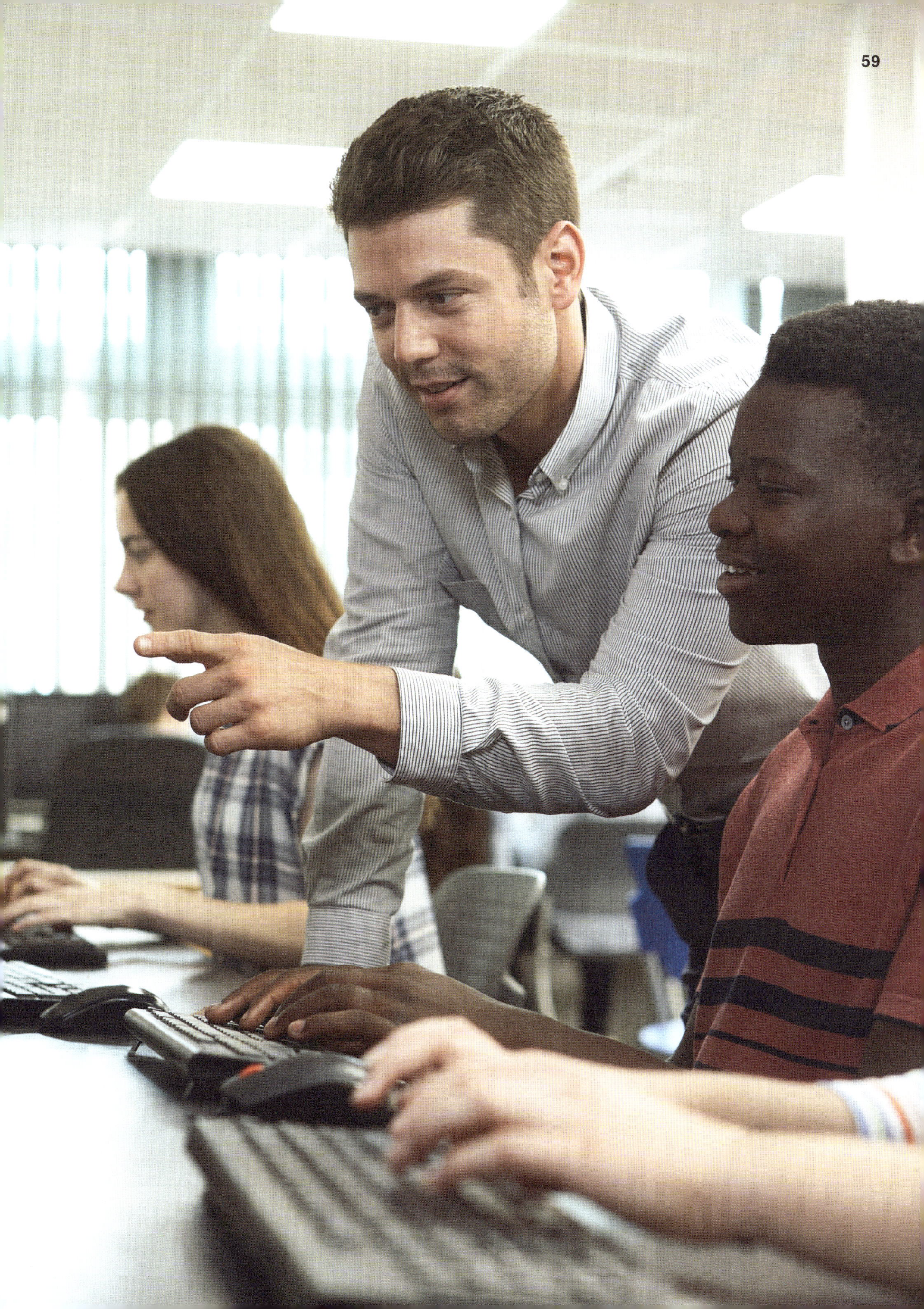

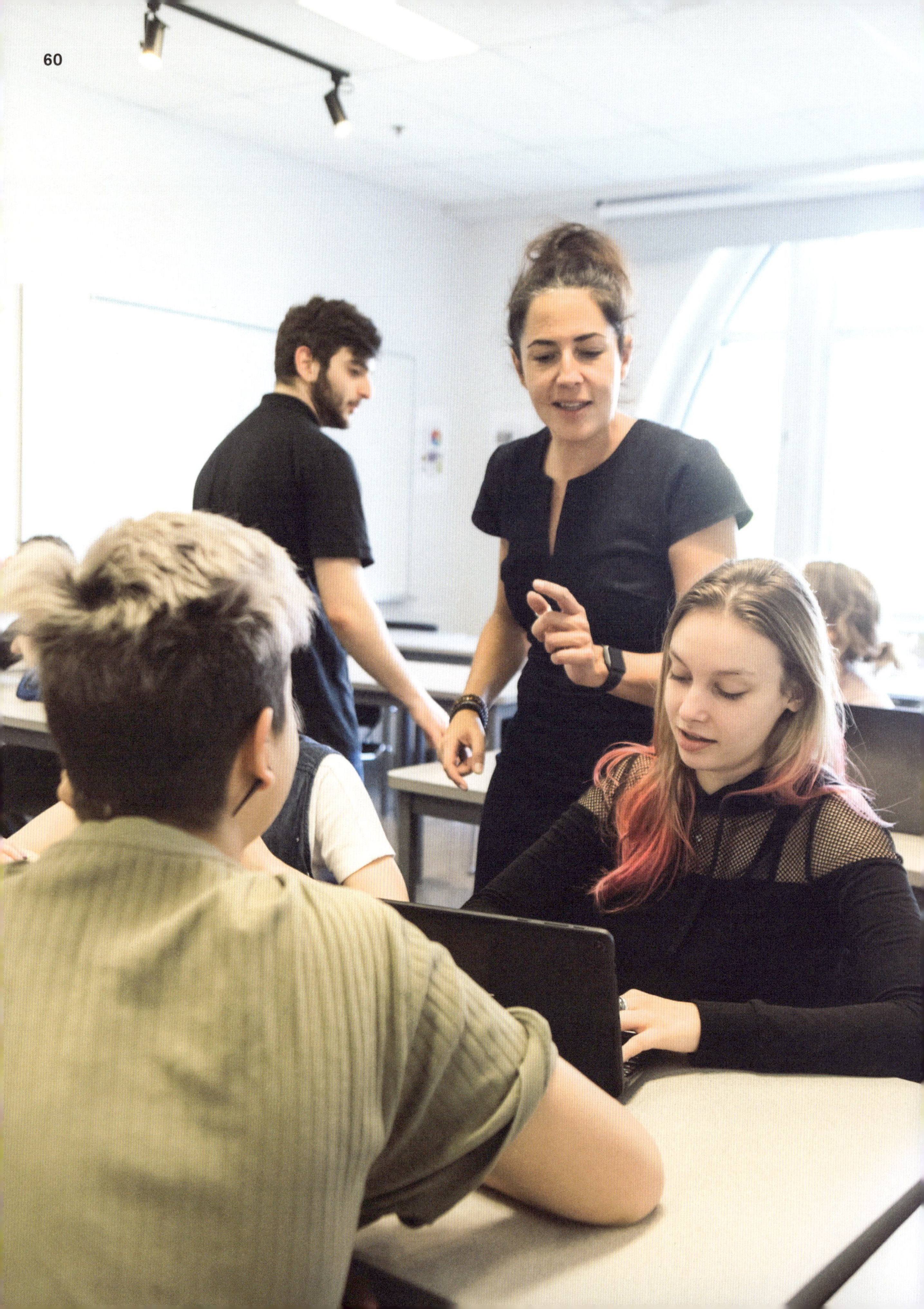

Section 5: Primary Initial Teacher Training respondents

A section of the survey asked questions about primary initial training providers and the barriers and benefits for engaging with schools. Primary trainee teachers are generally trained in all subjects that are taught in school, with computing being just one aspect of this.

How Primary ITT engage with schools

Between 11 and 13 respondents answered questions in this section of the survey. Over half of the respondents, 7 (54%), had more than 301 students in their cohort being placed each term. A third, 4 (31%) had only 1 to 50 being placed and 2 (16%) had between 51 and 150.

Respondents were asked what amount of time was allocated to training primary teachers on computing. 1 respondent said that computing was not explicitly covered, 2 respondents said that 2 to 3 hours of formal lectures were provided, 2 that 3 to 5 hours were provided, the majority 8 (62%) said that more than 5 hours were provided. 4 responded that as well as formal lectures schools were expected to cover computing for students. Participants were asked if the computing aspects of the ITT were formal credit-bearing or not, only 3 (23%) responded to say they were.

Barriers for Primary ITT to engaging with schools

Participants were asked what the barriers were for engaging with schools. They were given 7 possible reasons and an open ended response. For each reason they could select from a Likert scale of 1 to 5, with 1 the most significant important barrier and 5 the least. 1 "This stops me completely" to 5 "This is not a barrier". We have grouped responses 1 and 2, and 3 and 4 to simplify reporting.

As shown in Figure 13, the barriers which had been suggested in the survey were not reported as being significant by most respondents. One barrier was marginally more significant than the others, that of finding teachers who could support students. Only 1 of the 12 respondents (8%) reported that 6 of the suggested barriers either stopped them or were significant barriers.

Free-text responses to this question were interesting and raised several further issues and potential solutions.

One respondent explained that only a handful of schools in their area offered computing for older aged pupils so sometimes students had to be paired. Another raised the issue that computing provision varied greatly across schools. One participant raised the issue of the lack of staff to mentor students in school.

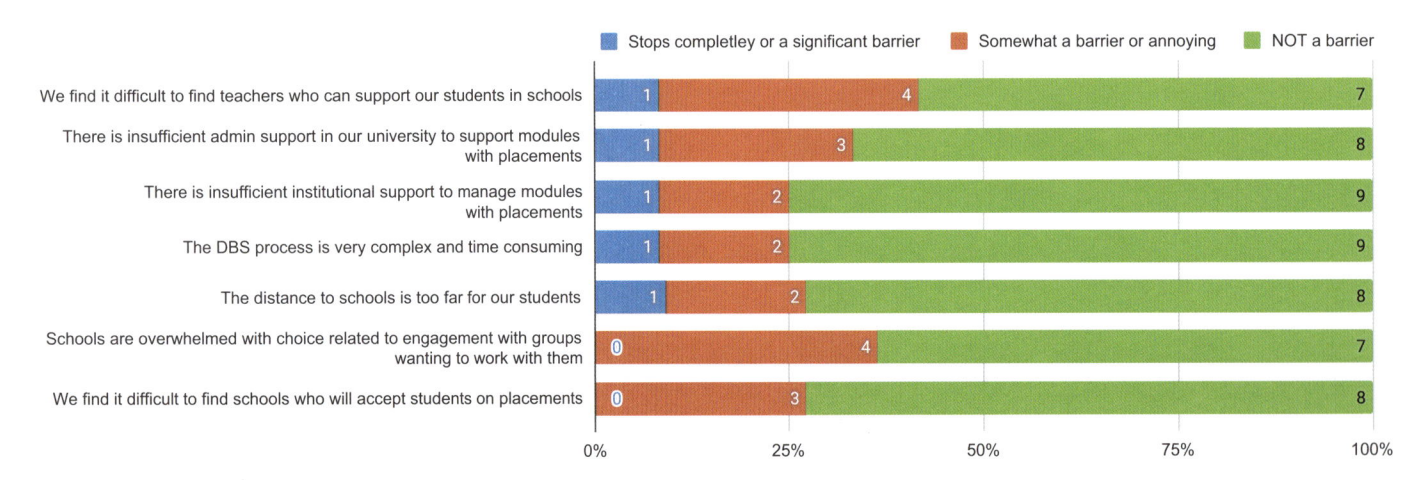

Figure 13: What are the barriers for Primary ITT for engaging with schools? (Click here for an interactive version of the chart)

An academic raised the issue of the wide range of computing provision in schools, this would impact student teachers experience of what good computing lessons might look like:

> "The provision for the teaching of computing in school varies." [Participant 141]

One respondent stated they had lots of schools with options to take trainees from many providers and another that they were in the opposite situation, as they covered a very wide area.

Participants were also asked how school engagement had changed over time.

Several raised the issue of COVID-19 impacting placements. Another mentioned that ITT funding in schools is decreasing and impacting on career changers. 3 responded that they were finding it easier to find placements in schools now, a reason given was that there is a shortage of staff and senior leadership are on the look out for good trainees to offer jobs to.

This was exemplified by one academic:

> "It is easier now. Schools are short staffed and finding recruitment tricky. Anecdotally several HTs <head teachers> have told me they are hoping to find good students to recruit quickly before other schools take them." [Participant 120]

When asked whether they were considering undertaking research only 2 affirmed they might, one a PhD and the other a non qualification classroom based research and potentially an EdD[87].

Summary of barriers and suggestions of opportunities to overcome these

In summary, for Primary ITT, the focus is not on computing alone as primary teachers are generalists and computing is one subject along with many others. Cohort sizes are generally large, over 300 students. The provision of training on computing varied significantly, from none to over 5 hours of lectures and support from schools. During placements the provision for trainees gaining experience in teaching computing is similarly variable, with ITT providers finding it difficult to access schools with computing being offered, or with school mentors who can support trainees' development in this area. However, placements in general are not difficult to find.

---

[87] https://teach.com/online-ed/education-degrees/edd-vs-phd/

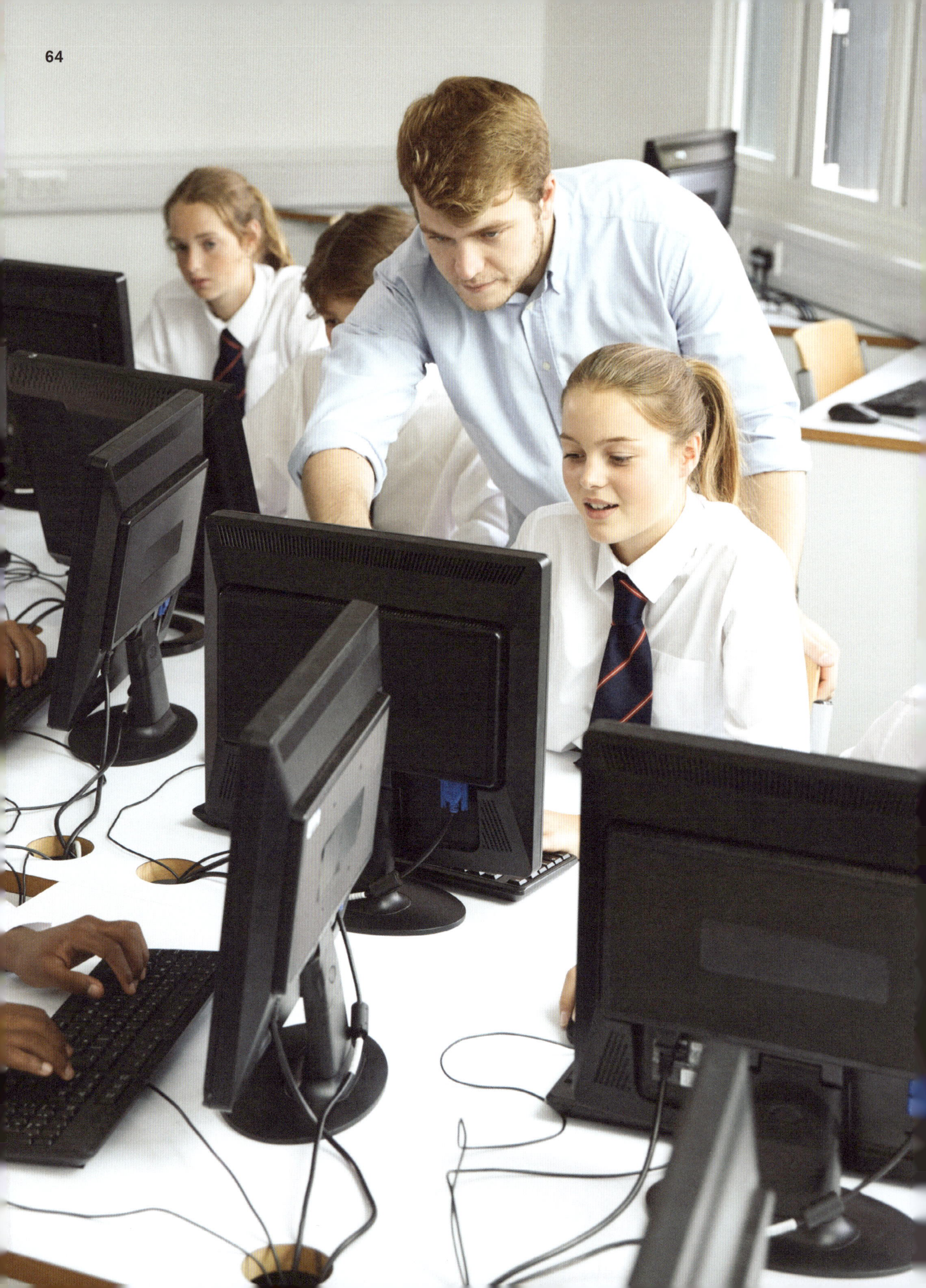

Section 6: Secondary Initial Teacher Training respondents

A section of the survey asked questions about secondary initial training providers and the barriers and benefits for engaging with schools. Secondary trainee teachers are subject-specific, only trained in one subject.

How Secondary ITT engage with schools

Only 5 to 6 participants responded to the questions in this section. Usually universities have a small cohort of secondary computing trainees. We were very surprised to see one respondent say that they had 900 ITT teachers studying computer science at their institution, but we suspect that this includes teachers of all disciplines rather than just computer science. Of the other 5 participants, 1 said they had 1 to 10 trainee teachers, 2 said 11 to 20 trainees and 2 had 21 to 30 trainees.

Participants were asked how computing is covered for students. Responses included university days with lectures, study time, tutorials, credit-bearing assignments, pre-course subject knowledge enhancement, action research during placements, weekly subject pedagogy days, developing and evaluating delivered schemes of work and students working as staff in schools.

Three example responses for the question on how computing was covered are shown:

> "We have a subject specialist team for primary and secondary. We also have a pre course SKE <subject knowledge enhancement> for 8 weeks for any with particular knowledge gaps Action research in the classroom linked to subject specific assignments." [Participant 92]

> "Gosh, huge question! We have a weekly subject pedagogy day which has a curriculum/ topic focus. Written assignments can have a subject focus. There are 3 written assignments. The third involves developing a scheme of work, teaching it and assessing its success at overcoming a specific learning barrier. Teacher standard 3 is assessed through placement evidence and reflections relating to the Monday subject sessions." [Participant 108]

> "1 year PGCE course including 2 days per week University based teaching and 3 days per week block placement for the whole year. University days comprise 4 x 3 hour lectures / seminars, 1 x 1 hour study time and 1 x 1 hour tutorial and support time. On placement students are expected to act and be treated as full time members of staff with a 75% teaching load." [Participant 86]

Barriers for Secondary ITT to engaging with schools

As with Primary ITT respondents, Secondary ITT respondents were asked about barriers to engaging with schools. The same questions were asked to both groups.

Participants were asked what the barriers were for engaging with schools, they were given 7 possible reasons and an open ended response. For each reason they could select from a Likert scale of 1 to 5, with 1 the most important barrier and 5 the least (1 "This stops me completely" to 5 "This is not a barrier".) We have grouped responses 1 and 2, and 3 and 4 to simplify reporting.

As shown in Figure 14, in general the responses were less positive than Primary ITT to the barriers suggested. However, the number of respondents was very small. Finding schools to place students, finding teachers to support students in school and universities having insufficient administration to support placements were mentioned as being either a significant barrier or somewhat of a barrier by over half, 3, (60%) of the respondents.

As with Primary ITT responses interesting findings were derived from the free-text responses. The main difficulty highlighted was the barrier of not having teachers who could mentor students in schools.

Schools and universities, how do they work together to support the teaching and learning of computing?

Barrier	Stops completely or a significant barrier	Somewhat a barrier or annoying	NOT a barrier
We find it difficult to find schools who will accept students on placements	1	2	2
We find it difficult to find teachers who can support our students in schools	1	2	2
There is insufficient admin support in our university to support modules with placements	1	2	2
The distance to schools is too far for our students	0	3	2
There is insufficient institutional support to manage modules with placements	0	2	3
The DBS process is very complex and time consuming	0	2	3
Schools are overwhelmed with choice related to engagement with groups wanting to work with them	0	2	3

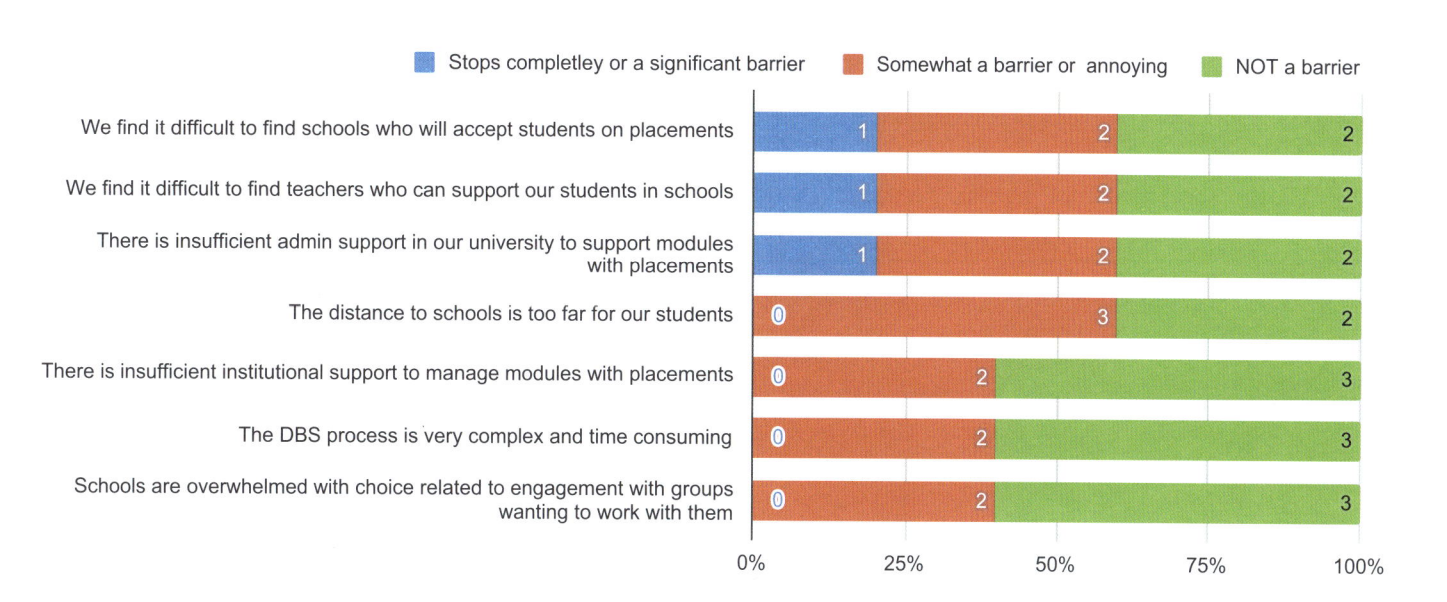

Figure 14: What are the barriers for Secondary ITT to engaging with schools? (Click here for an interactive version of the chart)

One academic covered most of other respondents points in his free-text comment saying:

> "Schools are approached by more than one University in the area, Universities work to different calendar dates, Universities set different assignments, schools are reluctant to offer places as they feel threatened due to lack of own subject knowledge in departments, schools have not offered a placement in a number of years despite us contacting them directly, lack of computing teaching is a concern in some schools – we can't place student teachers in these schools". [Participant 144]

Another respondent raised a significant issue that schools reject specific students rather than the placement:

> "Some placement schools want to interview trainees before offering them a placement. In September, even we don't really know the trainees very well so this is a worry for the trainees. Some schools then decline the offer which is a real vote of no confidence in them." [Participant 108]

When asked if things had changed over time, there was a mixed response, with some respondents saying things had got better and others saying it had got worse. One responded that since the change from IT to CS, it was now more difficult to find places for students. Another said as they were a "local contact", and because of outreach, things were better in terms of finding placements, but because they have more trainees now, they need more schools and this is an issue. An academic summarised this clearly:

> "Yes, it is getting harder to place students. Professional mentors (PMs) in schools will not always work with Subject mentors who offer us a place, then the PM stops it from happening. This has increased. Some schools who we had good working relationships do not engage with the department, stating no time to support a trainee teacher on their time allocation or towards their annual PDR <(Performance and Development Review)> so they see no point in supporting us." [Participant 144]

Summary of barriers and suggestions of opportunities to overcome these

In summary, for Secondary ITT, the focus is on computing, secondary teachers are subject specialists and the experience they have with relation to both pedagogy for teaching computing and subject knowledge compared to primary is significant. Cohort sizes are generally small, less than 30. The provision of training on computing was relatively consistent in terms of lectures, assignments and research informed experiences. However, as with Primary ITT, there are difficulties with placements. ITT providers find it difficult to find schools with computing being offered, or with school mentors who can support trainees. Placements, unlike in primary, are difficult to find, with ITT's competing for the same schools and schools being selective in terms of reviewing and being able to reject the students who are being proposed to be sent. One respondent suggested that forming personal relationships with schools, as the "local contact" and through outreach could help with finding placements.

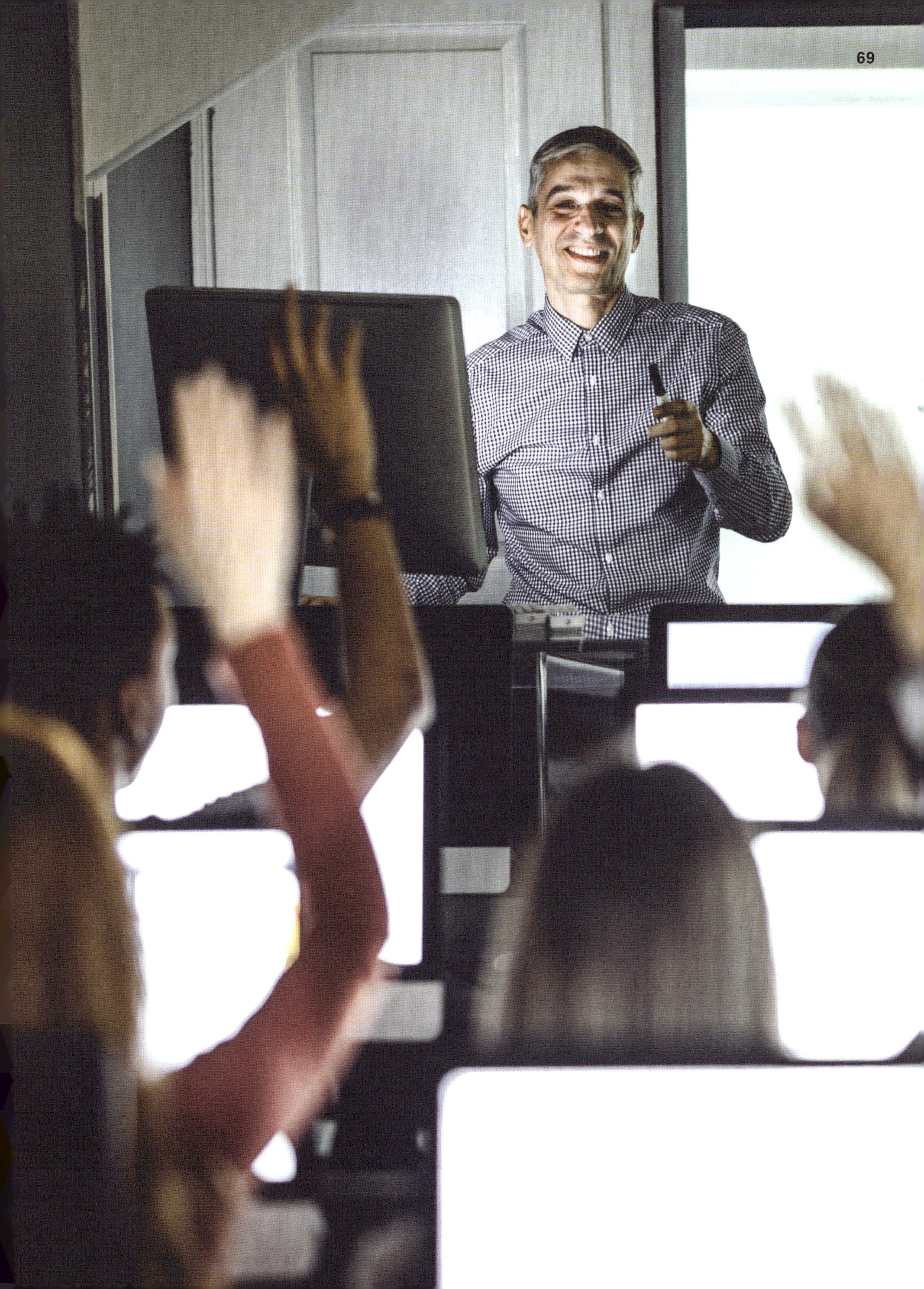

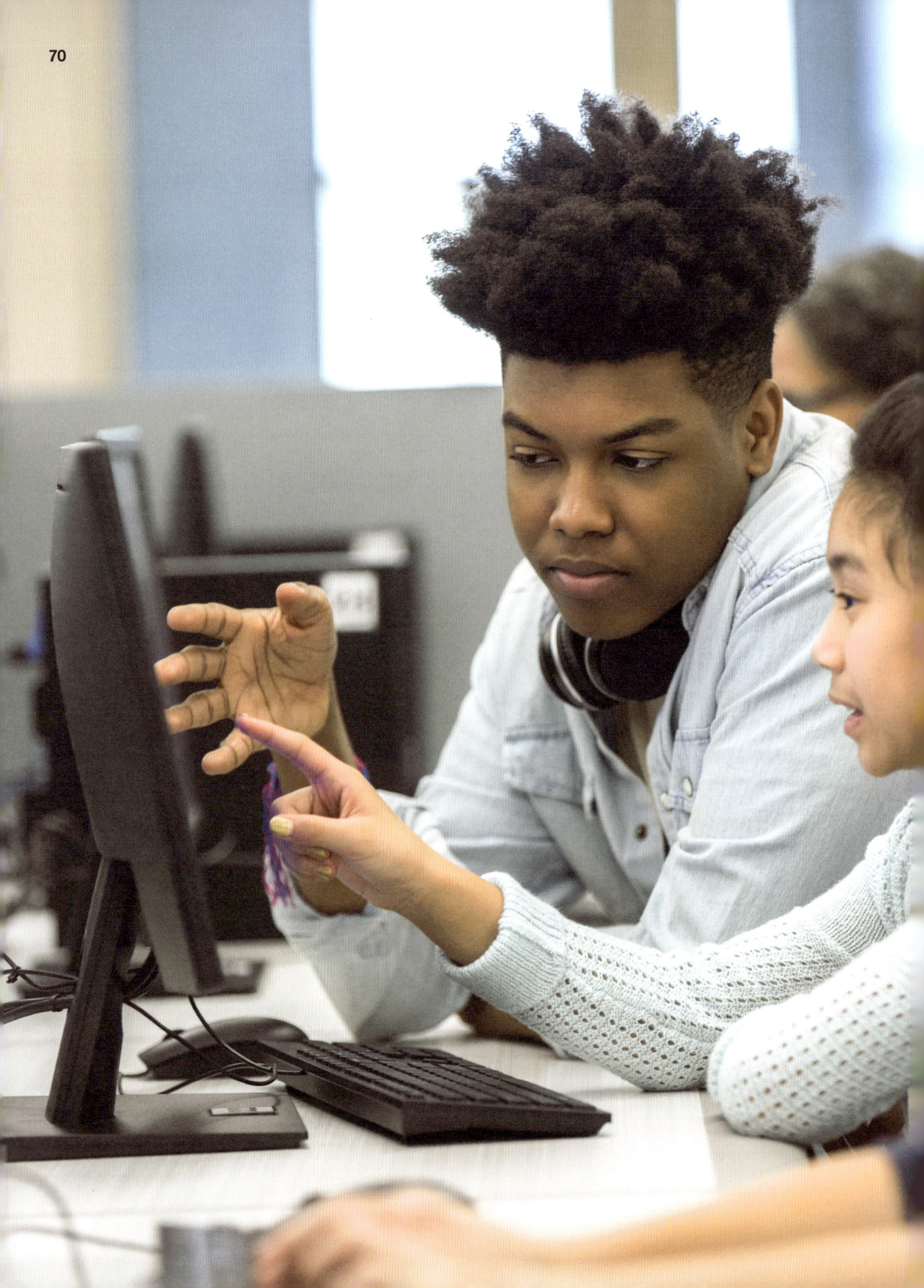

Appendices

Appendix A
Large scale computing education initiatives and landscape overview in the four nations of UK

In response to calls for further investment to support computing teaching [88], significant UK government investment has been allocated to a large scale programme of teacher training and resource development. In England, this programme is run by the National Centre for Computing Education (NCCE) and is being delivered through a new school-based hub structure. In Wales, teacher training and support for computing has been provided through a university-led model, Technocamps, established since 2003. In Northern Ireland professional development is often delivered through the universities and university colleges supported by either the Dept of Education, Education Authority https://www.eani.org.uk/[89] or the Dept for the Economy. In Scotland, teacher training for computing is provided through a university-led model by some of the Initial Teacher Education (ITE) providers. However, support for in-service teachers is decentralised and includes a variety of grassroots groups, government-funded and third-sector organisations. There are also online communities and continuous lifelong professional learning targeted at different stages and areas of the Computing curriculum in different local authority areas and online sites.

A new landscape of centralised teacher to teacher support in computing is unfolding in England whereas support in Wales and Northern Ireland generally remains University centred. Scotland has a mix of university led Computing initial teacher education combined with a more decentralised system of support for inservice teachers with the Scottish Qualifications Authority, Education Scotland and Skills Development Scotland each funding and signposting a range of different national Computing professional learning resources and events. The key CPD providers for each nation are summarised in the Table 1 below.

---

88 https://royalsociety.org/~/media/policy/projects/computing-education/computing-education-report.pdf
89 https://www.eani.org.uk/

Table 1: Key CPD provider by region

Nation	Large scale computing education initiatives and landscape overview
Wales	There are eight universities across Wales: Aberystwyth University, Bangor University, Cardiff University, Cardiff Metropolitan University, Glynd r University, Swansea University, University of South Wales, and University of Wales Trinity St David. Each of these universities has a Computer Science Department, and each of these is home to a *Technocamps* hub. Founded in 2003, Technocamps is a universities-based schools and community outreach operation which facilitates the direct engagement of the universities with schools, school children and their teachers through various programmes. It initially concentrated on providing workshops to secondary school students, but expanded its primary school engagement with the introduction of its *Playground Computing* programme in 2011, and its teacher CPD programme with the introduction of its *Technoteach* programme in 2012. Instrumental in the 2013 *Independent Review of the ICT Curriculum* commissioned by the Welsh Government, Technocamps led in reforming the subject of ICT, and in defining and implementing a new statutory bilingual *Digital Competence Framework (DCF)* for all pupils in Wales aged 3 to 16. In particular, Technocamps led on embedding the DCF in schools by delivering 10 hours of workshops in each of 97% of the nation's secondary schools. Since 2016 the DCF has been the primary mechanism of developing cross-curricular digital skills for all pupils in all Welsh schools. Technocamps was instrumental in supporting a 2018 sector review of ICT qualifications in Wales, resulting in the creation of innovative GCSE and A-Level qualifications in *Digital Technology*, for first teaching in 2021. Technocamps has engaged deeply – its standard programme being four full days of activity – with over 60,000 young people since 2011 (8% of the Welsh population today aged 5-24, with a near-even gender balance) to create an interest in the subject, particularly amongst young girls to address a desperately under-represented community in the digital workforce. Through its Technoteach programme of teacher CPD, Technocamps has delivered a year-long Level-3 accredited *Certificate in the Teaching of Computing* to over 100 teachers across Wales, as well as provided extensive support and resources to far greater numbers of teachers. (See Appendix E for more detail on Technocamps and the computing education landscape in Wales)

Nation	Large scale computing education initiatives and landscape overview
Northern Ireland	There are four universities/university colleges in Northern Ireland. The Computing university departments within Queen's University Belfast and Ulster University are of comparable size and both deliver events for schools and professional development at Level 7 (Post graduate Certificate). These are supported by the Department for the Economy. The Further Education Colleges also provide training and events for schools through their computing departments. Stranmillis University College and St Mary's University College similarly support the computing agenda through the Education Authority NI https://www.eani.org.uk/.

Queen's University Belfast (QUB), with a Dept of Computer Science and Software Engineering, supplies a range of showcase events, professional development courses for secondary teachers and taster days. In June 2017 the Computer Science Department in QUB formally came under the umbrella of Computing At School. A small number of professional development events which they deliver are CAS events.

Ulster University has a Computer Science Dept which is on a split campus site – Magee Campus, Derry and Jordanstown Campus. Ulster University supplies a range of support events for schools, professional development and showcase events. This is often done through their Widening Participation Programme.

Stranmillis University College is a college of QUB. It holds the Chair of CAS(NI), it is the seat of the Barefoot Computational Thinking resources alignment to the NI Curriculum and is the regional academic centre for Digital SchoolHouse which currently has 8 Lead Schools and is supporting almost 25% of the primary schools in Northern Ireland. It delivers the professional development courses in primary computational thinking and computing for the Education Authority of Northern Ireland through their Shared Education Programme. Stranmillis University College does not have a specific computer science department though it delivers computing to its ITE students. While computing in the primary schools in Northern Ireland remains non compulsory the route taken by schools can be towards Digital Literacy rather than computing and computational thinking.

St Mary's University College is a sister college to Stranmillis and is also a college of QUB. It delivers computing through its teacher education courses and promotes CAS events to its students. |

Nation	Large scale computing education initiatives and landscape overview
Scotland	In Scotland, there are eleven university providers of Initial Teacher Education accredited by the General Teaching Council for Scotland, five of which offer either an undergraduate or postgraduate degree programme in Secondary Computing teaching The University of: Edinburgh, Glasgow, Strathclyde, the West of Scotland and Stirling. All Initial Teacher Education Primary teaching providers should also provide suitable experiences to develop their students' understanding of key issues across the eight curricular areas in Curriculum for Excellence, including Computing Science, a distinct context within the area of Technologies. Over the last fifteen years there has also been a steady stream of national projects and joint work to support school level computing education by university schools of computing including: CSInside[90]; The Royal Society of Edinburgh and BCS Computing Science Exemplification project [91], Professional Learning And Networking for Computing[92] feedback on the development of the SQA Curriculum for Excellence Computing Science qualifications and a new reference language for examinations[93], work with Education Scotland to redevelop the Computing Science Experiences and Outcomes and benchmarks within the revised Technologies curricular area[94]; The Data Education in Schools project[95], 2018-2026; research for Skills Development Scotland into Computing teacher supply issues[96], and a series of 2021 articles with education research informed Computing Science teaching advice for Education Scotland's new Digilearn:Computing Science pathway. From its founding in 2011 until it became largely dormant in 2018, Computing At Schools Scotland organised national conferences, local events, developed guides and resources for teachers and advocated for the importance of school Computing. More recently, in 2020, the BCS established a Scottish Computing Education Committee with representatives from university, industry and third sector organisations to coordinate support and provide advice on strategic direction and future needs of Computing education at all levels. A new grassroots teacher-led group called Computing Science Scotland has also emerged aiming to provide support for Computing teachers. *Continued*

90   Quintin Cutts, Margaret Brown, Lynsey Kemp & Calum Matheson, 2007, Enthusing and informing potential computer science students and their teachers in ACM SIGSCE Bulletin, 39(3), 196-200. https://doi.org/10.1145/1269900.1268842
91   Jeremy Scott, 2013, The royal society of Edinburgh/British computer society computing science exemplification project, ITiCSE'13, 315 https://doi.org/10.1145/2462476.2465574
92   Quintin Cutts, Judy Robertson, Peter Donaldson, Laurie O'Donnell, 2017, An evaluation of a professional learning network for computer science teachers in Journal of Computer Science Education, 27 (1), 30-35 https://doi.org/10.1080/08993408.2017.1315958
93   https://www.sqa.org.uk/sqa/48477.html
94   Richard Connor, Quintin Cutts & Judy Robertson, 2017, Keeping the machinery in computing education in Communications of the ACM, 60(11), 26-28 http://dx.doi.org/10.1145/3144174
95   Tommy Lawson & Judy Robertson, 2020, Building Digital Technology Capacity to Support Data Education in Edinburgh and South East Scotland Region Schools: Summary and Recommendations, Commissioned by Edinburgh and South East Scotland City Region Deal - DDI Skills Gateway. https://www.research.ed.ac.uk/en/publications/building-digital-technology-capacity-to-support-data-education-in
96   Judy Robertson, 2019, Towards a sustainable solution for the shortage of computing teachers in Scotland, Commissioned by Skills Development Scotland https://www.research.ed.ac.uk/en/publications/towards-a-sustainable-solution-for-the-shortage-of-computing-teac

Nation	Large scale computing education initiatives and landscape overview
Scotland continued	Currently, the majority of sustained programmes of professional learning for in-service teachers are commissioned by either Education Scotland (ES), Skills Development Scotland (SDS) or the Scottish Qualifications Authority (SQA). Recent university-led work funded by these bodies includes an online additional teaching qualification in Secondary Computing[97] for teachers of other subjects by the University of the Highlands and Islands and a course for teachers by Abertay University to support the SQA's new National Progress Awards in Cyber Security[98] and related experiences and outcomes in the Broad General Education phase. Other major initiatives include: online Computing Science sessions and Computing Science- Gender lesson plans[99] by Education Scotland's Digital Learning team[100] and support for the Primary focused Barefoot Computing programme; the SQA's course on new elements of National 5 to Advanced Higher Computing Science[101] and Skills Development Scotland's Discover Cyber Skills initiative[102]. Further developments are likely in response to Mark Logan's Scottish technology ecosystem review[103] which identified that additional improvements in access to school level Computing education were necessary for future growth of the sector. Funding for extra-curricular Computing provision such as Codeclubs and competitions like the First Lego League is provided by the Digital Xtra Fund[104]. The Scottish Funding Council shared research pool SICSA (Scottish Informatics and Computing Science Alliance) also provides some funding to universities to support schools related events[105]. These often have associated professional learning for teachers and other adults supporting them. Within the Further Education sector each college has a designated Computing lead who meet through events organised by the College Development Network[106]. Finally, University level Computing Education professional learning is supported by the SICSA Education director who oversees all events and developments for university lecturers in Scotland[107] in partnership with each institution's CS Education champion[108].

97 https://www.uhi.ac.uk/en/courses/cpd-award-additional-teaching-qual-in-computing-studies/
98 https://www.sqa.org.uk/sqa/74739.html
99 https://education.gov.scot/improvement/learning-resources/computing-science-gender-lesson-plans-resources-and-activities
100 https://blogs.glowscotland.org.uk/glowblogs/digilearn/
101 https://www.sqaacademy.org.uk/enrol/index.php?id=750
102 https://cyberskillslesson.com/
103 Mark Logan, 2020, Scottish technology ecosystem: review, Commissioned by the Scottish Government
   https://www.gov.scot/publications/scottish-technology-ecosystem-review/
104 https://www.digitalxtrafund.scot/
105 https://www.sicsa.ac.uk/education/education-event-sponsorship/
106 https://www.cdn.ac.uk/networks-projects/digitalnetworks/
107 https://www.sicsa.ac.uk/education/
108 https://www.sicsa.ac.uk/education/education-champions/

Nation	Large scale computing education initiatives and landscape overview
England	In England, Computer Science Departments in Universities have long championed and supported the teaching of computer science in schools. This has included providing teacher professional development, pupil facing lessons and producing resources for schools both for teaching lessons and for classroom displays. Representative bodies such as the Council of Professors and Heads of Computing (CPHC)[109], the BCS, the Chartered Institute for IT professionals[110], and Computing at School [111] have led initiatives lobbying for the inclusion of computer science in schools and to support development of computing education in schools. To support professional development of computing educators working in HE the CPHC coordinates initiatives and represents universities at a national level. Computing At School[112], known as CAS, is a grassroots organisation of computing educators from school, university and informal settings. It works to increase the profile of computer science education and improve the quality of provision. Working across educational sectors CAS has supported the relationship of universities and schools working together, for example, through programmes where some universities have coordinated communities of computing teachers and trained classroom teachers in computer science. The CAS Research and Universities Working Group specifically looks at matters related to schools and universities working together. Since 2018, the key CPD provider for school computing resources and classroom computing teachers in England has been the National Centre for Computing Education (NCCE)[113]. This is a large-scale, school-led, Department for Education programme which is coordinated and delivered by a consortium formed from STEM Learning[114], the Raspberry Pi Foundation[115], and BCS, The Chartered Institute for IT[116]. The NCCE has developed and delivered an extensive range of teacher training courses, classroom resources and teacher support for the delivery of computing in schools for learners from the age of 5 to 18. At the initial teacher training (ITT) stage of professional development, teachers are trained through a range of routes, including through university led courses and through school led routes, often called school-centred initial teacher training (SCITT). To support the teaching of computing to learners over the age of 18 the recent Institute of Coding (IoC)[117] project initially funded in 2018 by the Office of Students, brings together more than 35 universities and over 200 employers and industry bodies to encourage a larger and more diverse group of people onto tech careers through higher education, included in their work has been professional development for academics. (The IoC in Wales is a related but distinct HEFCW-funded project within Technocamps.)

109 https://cphc.ac.uk/
110 https://www.bcs.org/
111 https://www.computingatschool.org.uk/
112 https://www.computingatschool.org.uk/
113 https://teachcomputing.org/about
114 https://www.stem.org.uk/
115 https://www.raspberrypi.org/
116 https://www.bcs.org/
117 https://instituteofcoding.org/

Relationships between universities and schools can be influenced by third parties and external initiatives. For example, school pupil outreach events may be coordinated by the Royal Institution as part of their lecture series. Or a university might provide volunteers and a venue for competitions, such as the Lego League[118]. In-service teacher continuing professional development (CPD) might be developed by a third party and then delivered by universities as part of large scale national funded programmes e.g. NCCE accelerator programme, Technocamps. Or universities might develop and deliver local teacher CPD.

---

[118] https://www.firstlegoleague.org/

Appendix B

Survey respondents

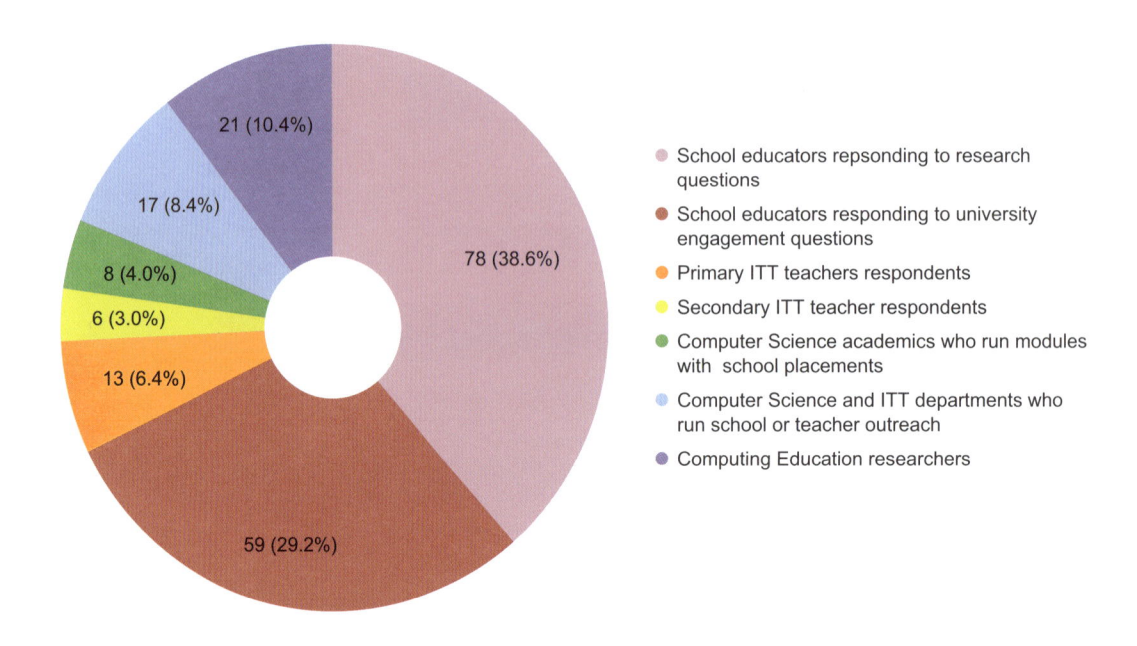

Figure 15: Survey Respondents per Survey Section

- School educators repsonding to research questions: 78 (38.6%)
- School educators responding to university engagement questions: 59 (29.2%)
- Primary ITT teachers respondents: 13 (6.4%)
- Secondary ITT teacher respondents: 6 (3.0%)
- Computer Science academics who run modules with school placements: 8 (4.0%)
- Computer Science and ITT departments who run school or teacher outreach: 17 (8.4%)
- Computing Education researchers: 21 (10.4%)

There were 6 sections for participants to complete about engagement between schools and universities. 143 respondents completed at least one section of the survey. As shown in Figure 1, 78 school teachers completed the section about research, 59 teachers completed questions about working with universities, 13 academics working in primary initial teacher training completed the section on working with schools, 6 academics working in secondary initial teacher training answered questions on working with schools, 8 academics from computer science departments who run undergraduate modules with school placements completed their section, 17 university academics who run run school outreach answered questions on working with schools and 21 computing education researchers completed the section on working with schools.

Of the 143 who completed one or more parts of the main survey, 112 completed the "About you" section which included questions on gender, where the respondent worked, ethnicity and disability. On the gender question, 58 (52%) reported female, 49 (44%) male and 5 (5%) did not want to declare (see Appendix F Table 2).

Regarding where the respondents taught or worked, the majority 90 (81%) reported they taught or worked in England, 10 (9%) in Wales, 7 (6%) in Scotland and no respondents selected Northern Ireland. 5 (4%) of respondents selected "Other" and went on to detail that 2 were from the US, 1 from Guyana, 1 from Singapore and 1 taught in England and Scotland (see Appendix F Table 4).

Schools and universities, how do they work together to support the teaching and learning of computing? 79

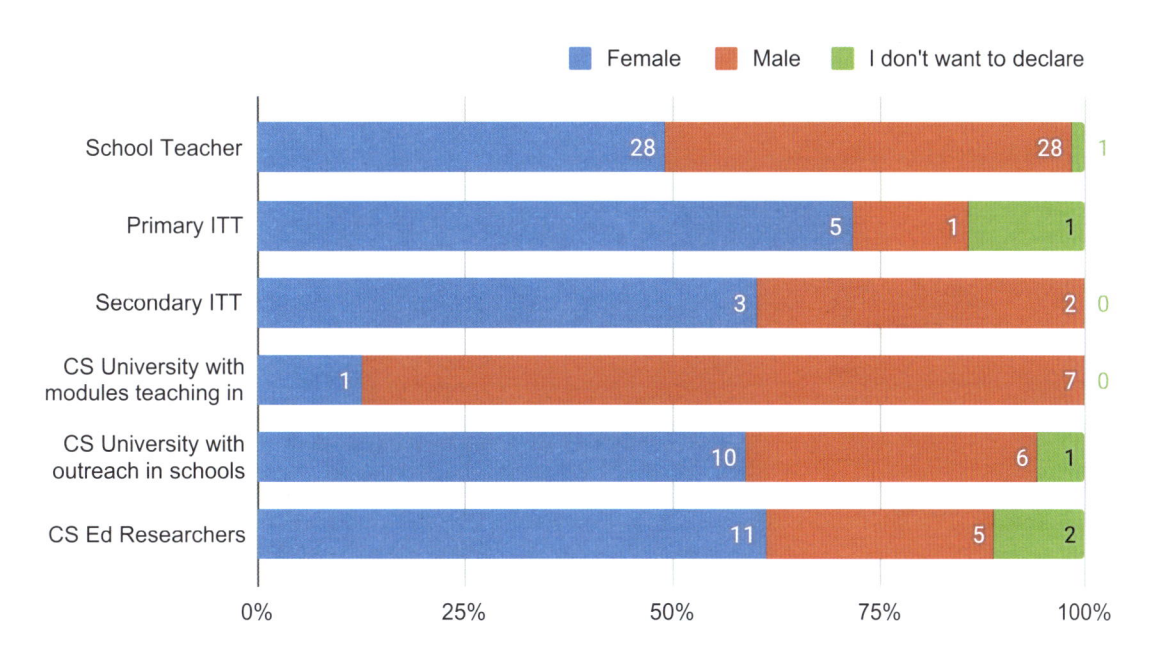

Figure 16: Respondents by stakeholder group and gender.

With reference to the question on Ethnicity, 74 (66%) of respondents reported as White, 15 (13%) as White – Scottish, Northern Irish, Welsh, English, 9(8%) did not want to declare, 3 (3%) as Black or Black British -African, 2 (2%) as White Irish, 2 (2%) as Other Mixed Background, 1 (1%) Asian or Asian British – Pakistani, 1 (1%) Other Asian background, 1 (1%) Mixed – White and Asian, 1 (1%) Asian or Asian British – Indian, 1 (1%) Chinese, 1 (1%) Other White background and 1 (1%) None (See Appendix F Table 5).

On the disability question, 89 (80%) of the 111 people answering this question reported having no known disability, 9 (8%) did not want to declare, 6 (5%) a specific learning difficulty such as dyslexia, dyspraxia and AD/HD, 3 (3%) a disability or impairment not listed, 2 (2%) as D/deaf or with a serious hearing impairment, 1 (1%) with a long standing illness or health condition, and 1 (1%) with a mental health condition.

With respect to how long participants had been involved in computing education, 57 (81%) of school stakeholders had 6 or more years experience teaching computing, 4 (57%) had similar in Primary ITT, 5 (100%) in Secondary ITT, 8 (100%) of those who run Computer Science modules including placements, 17 (82%) running Computer Science Outreach and 14 (78%) of computing education Researchers. Apart from Primary ITT at least 75% of participants had more than 6 years of experience teaching CS.

A set of questions were asked about membership and signup to various groups and newsletters, 84 (75%) of participants stated they were members of Computing At School[119], known as CAS, 60 (54%) said they received Hello World Magazines, 39 (35%) had signed up for the NCCE programme, 25 (22%) for the NCCE accelerator programme and 22 (20%) were members of the CAS Research Forum.

119   https://www.computingatschool.org.uk/

Appendix C

Survey questions

The survey was split into 6 sections, each for a different respondent role plus there was a general participant section.

The survey was for

- teachers in schools and informal settings of pupils aged 4 to 18 years old who teach computing or resource developers who make computing lesson resources for pupils aged 4 to 18 years old or professional development creators and delivery groups for computing teachers who teach pupils aged 4 to 18 years old
- primary initial teacher training staff including those working in schools and universities
- secondary computing initial teacher training staff including those working in schools and universities
- computer science university staff who run undergraduate modules which include school placements (such as Student Ambassadors)
- outreach university staff who run computing outreach for students or teachers (such as Lego League, Isaac Computing events)
- researchers undertaking computing education research

The survey could be completed more than once by a specific respondent if they had more than one role. A pdf of the questionnaire is available here[120].

As well as asking questions which were specific to each role, there were common repeated questions across roles such as:

1. What are the benefits from engaging? (Participants could respond by selecting from this is a most important benefit for me, this is an important benefit, this is somewhat of a benefit, this is a little benefit, this is not a benefit for me.)
2. What other benefits are there that we have not mentioned?
3. What are the barriers to engagement ? (Participants could respond by selecting from this stops me completely, this is a significant barrier, this is somewhat of a barriers, this is annoying but it does not stop me, this is not a barrier)
4. Tell us more about these barriers and any other barriers that we have not thought of.
5. Have the barriers changed over time? And if so how and why?

The participant section asked questions on items such as gender, region in which the participant worked, qualifications, length of time involved in computing education.

Ethics approval was obtained for the survey from Queen Mary University of London (QMUL), reference QMREC2419 and data was retained and processed in line with QMUL Data Policies. The anonymised data is available on request from the principal investigator J Waite (j.l.waite@qmul.ac.uk)

---

[120] https://teachinglondoncomputing.files.wordpress.com/2021/04/schooluniversityengagementsurvey2020.pdf

# Appendix D

Computing At School (CAS) and Universities

Computing at School[121], (CAS), is a grassroots community of teachers, academics and industry professionals who "lead and promote excellence in all those staff involved in Computing education in schools". CAS has a strategic alliance with BCS, The Chartered Institute of IT and is part of the BCS Academy.

Many CAS members are university educators and as of March 2021 a third of CAS Board members were university academics.

Some universities at some times have been central to CAS programmes of work. For example, from 2012 to 2018, the Department for Education funded the Network of Excellence[122]. The Network of Excellence aimed to inspire, motivate and support teachers by building a teacher professional development infrastructure nurturing collaboration between teachers, schools and universities. Ten CAS regional centres based in universities coordinated activity including running computing education conferences, providing teacher professional development, and co-ordinating the growth of computing educator communities. Historically, CAS has provided schools with a list of university contacts and encouraged collaboration between universities to support schools, for example, in sharing ideas on outreach and providing teacher training. The CAS website has also provided a mechanism for universities to advertise outreach events to schools both pupil and teacher-facing. With regard to research, CAS also gives university-based research communities opportunities to find schools and teachers to work with and there is a CAS Research (and Universities) Working Group that aims to champion computing education research and to support the relationship between schools and universities.

---

121   https://www.computingatschool.org.uk/
122   https://www.computingatschool.org.uk/custom_pages/35-noe#:~:text=The%20Network%20of%20Excellence%20(NoE,computing%20at%20the%20national%20level.

Appendix E

Technocamps and the Computing Education Landscape in Wales

The Computer Science Departments in the various Universities throughout Wales have a long history of collaborative activity undertaking industrial and educational outreach. This began in earnest with the creation of *ITWales* in 1993. This programme flourished, with the membership of its business club numbering over 1500 and an average of 850 unique visitors each day to its monthly online business magazine.

An independent review of ITWales by Welsh Government (Kingsley Stock AIBA, 2006) noted *"ITWales has developed a very impressive and proven model of collaboration between business and the universities. It is a unique model that can be replicated into any discipline and expanded into other universities. The universities should examine this model and consider embedding it into its industrial liaison activities."* The 2006 EPSRC International Review of ICT noted *"ITWales successful outreach programme has matured to a state that exceeds the informal funding available thus far."* At a Technology Futures Conference on 13 November 2007, Mike Rodd (BCS Director) pined *"If only there was an ITWales in England!"*

As the world became ever more digital, the demand for computing skills in the workplace grew. Unfortunately, the appeal of computer studies in schools waned – along with the competence to teach it – as a creative computer science curriculum was slowly replaced by a more mundane ICT curriculum. It became apparent to ITWales that its greatest contribution to the businesses of the future would be to ensure the pipeline of talent that it would rely on by tackling the problems of computing education in schools.

Technocamps[123] was created in 2003 as an ITWales programme to do just this. Its initial aim was to provide interactive workshops introducing secondary school children to the world of computing which they were not seeing in school. The ambition was to change any negative preconceptions about the subject that the young people might have developed, and thus create a demand from the children that would spread to their parents, teachers and schools. We have made great strides in the intervening 18 years; but the problems we need to overcome are great. And they are universal: there are many organisations and governments across the world that are waking up to the problems in computing education in schools and addressing these problems with various initiatives.

Solving the problems requires much more than engaging with and enthusing the children. What is needed is a multi-faceted approach which does this as well as upskill both the teaching professionals responsible for inspiring and educating young people, and those who are currently employed in businesses that are becoming ever more reliant on technology. This realisation has led to the expansion of the Technocamps programme to the point where it has absorbed – and thus become – the ITWales mission.

Crucially, it remains a wholly universities-based operation. Based at Swansea University, it has a hub in the computer science department in every university across Wales. Due to its model of direct and sustained engagement, it relies on substantial external funding; but the universities contribute much in-kind, and everything it offers is free to the participants.

Apart from the secondary-focussed Technocamps workshops, it has three further strands: *Playground Computing*, a primary-school engagement programme founded in 2011; *Technoteach*, a teacher CPD programme founded in 2012; and the *Institute of Coding in Wales*, an industry engagement programme. It also has a broad-themed research arm at Swansea University under the title *Educational, Historical and Philosophical Foundations of Computer Science*.

[123] https://www.technocamps.ac.uk/

Appendix F

Data

Anonymised data is available on request from Jane Waite j.l.waite@qmul.ac.uk

Table 2: Stakeholders responding to each section in the survey

Survey Section	Number of respondents answering questions in this section
School educators responding to research questions	78
School educators responding to university engagement questions	59
Primary initial teacher training respondents answering school engagement questions	13
Secondary initial teacher training respondents answering school engagement questions	6
Computer Science academics who run modules with school placements responding to school engagement questions	8
Computer Science and ITT departments who run school or teacher outreach responding to school engagement questions	17
Computing Education researchers responding to school engagement questions	21
Total respondents across all sections	202
Total respondents: Note the school educators were the same participants for sections on research and university engagement	143

Table 3: Stakeholders responding by Gender

	Female	Male	I don't want to declare	Total
School Teacher	28	28	1	57
Primary ITT	5	1	1	7
Secondary ITT	3	2	0	5
CS University with modules teaching in schools	1	7	0	8
CS University with outreach in schools	10	6	1	17
CS Ed Researchers	11	5	2	18
	58	49	5	112
%	52%	44%	4%	

Table 4: Stakeholders responding by Region

	England	Scotland	Ireland	Wales	Other Please specify		Total
School Teacher	47	0	0	8	2	Singapore, England and Scotland	57
Primary ITT	7	0	0	0	0		7
Secondary ITT	5	0	0	0	0		5
CS University with modules teaching in schools	5	2	0	1	0		8
CS University with outreach in schools	15	1	0	1	0		17
CS Ed Researchers	11	4	0	0	3	Guyana, US, US New York	18
	90	7	0	10	5		112
%	80%	6%	0%	9%	4%		

Table 5: Stakeholder responding by Ethnic

	School Teacher	Primary ITT	Secondary ITT	CS University with modules teaching in schools	CS University with outreach in schools	CS Ed Researchers	Total	%
White	40	4	3	6	12	9	74	66%
White – Scottish, Northern Irish, Welsh, English	9	0	1	2	1	2	15	13%
Asian or Asian British – Pakistani	1	0	0	0	0	0	1	1%
I don't want to declare	3	1	0	0	2	3	9	8%
Chinese	1	0	0	0	0	0	1	1%
Other – Asian background	1	0	0	0	0	0	1	1%
White – Irish	1	0	0	0	0	1	2	2%
None	1	0	0	0	0	0	1	1%
Black – or Black British – African	0	2	0	0	0	1	3	3%
Other – Mixed background	0	0	1	0	1	0	2	2%
Mixed – White and Asian	0	0	0	0	1	0	1	1%
Asian – or Asian British – Indian	0	0	0	0	0	1	1	1%
Other – White background	0	0	0	0	0	1	1	1%
	57	7	5	8	17	18	112	